TO DIE FOR THE PEOPLE

THE WRITINGS OF HUEY P. NEWTON

EDITED BY TONI MORRISON

TO DIE FOR THE PEOPLE

THE WRITINGS OF
HUEY P. NEWTON

EDITED BY TONI MORRISON

Writers and Readers

Writers and Readers Publishing, Inc., New York

Writers and Readers Publishing, Inc.
P.O. Box 461, Village Station
New York, NY 10014

c/o Airlift Book Company
26-28 Eden Grove
London N7 8EF England

Cover Design: Terrie Dunkelberger

Published by Random House, 1972
This edition published by Writers and Readers Publishing, Inc., 1995

ISBN: 0-86316-327-0

1 2 3 4 5 6 7 8 9 0

To the fallen comrades
of the Black Panther Party

To die for the . . . racists . . . is lighter than a feather. But to die for the people . . . is heavier than any mountain and deeper than any sea.

—HUEY P. NEWTON

ACKNOWLEDGMENTS

To all those who contributed so generously so I could have the time, the place, the quiet and the space to work on this and other works.

Without the help of the Black Panther Party, Dr. Herman Blake, Franz Schurmann, Martin Kenner, my brother Melvin Newton, Donald Freed, and my editor Toni Morrison, this book would not have been possible.

To the editor of the *Black Panther Intercommunal News Service* and Minister of Information Comrade Elaine Brown, to the late Comrade Samuel L. Napier, Circulation Manager, and to my secretary Gwen V. Fountaine, typist, Delois Burbie, and to my good friend Burt Schneider, whose generous encouragement greatly aided me in difficult times, my sincere thanks for their assistance.

CONTENTS

Introduction

In the latter decades of the eighteenth century, three great revolutions took place. In America, a colony achieved independence. In Britain, the industrial revolution turned an empire into a world market system based on the capitalist mode of production. In France, oppressed classes rose and destroyed an oppressor class. The currents generated by these revolutions formed a revolutionary process which now has reached the entire world. All colonies demand independence to become nations. All nations seek a mode of production to give themselves wealth and power. All peoples who suffer oppression, exploitation, and inequality through class struggle seek liberty, equality, and fraternity.

As these three currents spread outward from America, Britain, and France, they intermingled but also, thereby, generated contradictions. Colonies fought for and secured independence, but then lost it again to empires armed with the weapons of capitalism. Capitalism produced immense wealth but created new class inequalities based on exploitation and oppression. In the middle of the nineteenth century, Karl Marx and Friedrich Engels developed a theory of socialism to resolve the contradiction of capitalism and class struggle: the oppressed classes led by the vanguard of the industrial proletariat will seize power, form the workers' state through the abolition of private property, and so do away with the basis of class distinctions to create a mode of production for, through, and by the people. Out of this theory came the vision of Vladimir Lenin, the revolutionary practice of the Bolshevik Party, and the Russian Revolution.

In the twentieth century, China, an immense country subject to the oppression of feudalism, the exploitation of empire capitalism, and the racism of White men, underwent a revolution mightier than that of Russia. Under the leadership of the soldier and intellectual Mao Tse-tung, the Communist Party of China smashed all of China's oppressor classes, freed China from alien empires, and gave the Chinese people the dignity and authority of masters in their own house. Out of a half-century of struggle before and after the seizure of power, Mao Tse-tung rediscovered the fact that revolution is a process and not a conclusion, that contradictions continue to generate struggle even after revolutionaries have seized power. This is so because new forms of oppression keep on arising (like the bureaucratic dictatorship which the Chinese people overthrew in their recent Cultural Revolution), for the existence of any empire is by itself a contradiction, because so long as there are colonized peoples anywhere in the world they will make war to achieve their freedom.

By the middle of the twentieth century, it has become clear that the honor of being fighters in the revolutionary process belongs not just to the big nations. Everywhere in Asia, Africa, and Latin America, colonies have achieved independence, and independent nations are struggling to cast off empires. And in independent nations the poor are rising to cast off newer forms of imperialist, neo-colonialist, and native bourgeois domination. The greatest of these Third World revolutions is the struggle of the Vietnamese people against the greatest empire in human history, the United States of America. First, the city people of Vietnam achieved independence from French rule. Then the peasants of Vietnam threw off the shackles of landlord oppression. Now, all Vietnamese fight to throw out of their country an alien American occupier bloated with dollars, festooned with weapons, who regards their country as a testing ground of his ability to maintain his clutches on the rest of the world.

While the revolutionary process spread outward from

America, Britain, and France, it also flowed back into those countries. In Britain, class struggle continued through the nineteenth century and independence movements battered its empire in the twentieth century. But most important for its own people, Britain was reduced to its natural state as an off-shore island by alien capitalist empires who greedily sought what Britain already had—first Germany who wanted to take it by force and then America who inherited it by default. In France, class struggle raged in the nineteenth century, but competing with the poor for power was a still revolutionary capitalism which did not finally win until the twentieth century. In contrast to Britain and France, America in the nineteenth century appeared as a place of hope for the revolutionary process. America encouraged and supported colonial independence movements. Its capitalism was the most dynamic, aggressive, and creative in the world, attracting millions of immigrants. And class struggle achieved a sublime form in the Civil War which appeared as a struggle for the emancipation of Black people: the poorest, most oppressed, most exploited people in the world.

By the end of the nineteenth century, reactionary forces who were determined to end once and for all the revolutionary process—that struggle of the poor for power, equality, and justice—gained sway. America began toying with the idea of empire when it seized Spain's remnant colonies in the Caribbean and the Far East. Its hard-driving capitalists turned into a new ruling class interested primarily in power and wealth for themselves and their "middle-class" allies. And they decided that the poor had to be kept in their place forever, so signifying by reintroducing slavery for Black people in the form of "segregation." The empire became a global reality in 1945 when America, rich and unscathed, picked up the wreckage of World War II. Join the empire, America's rulers said, and you will have a share in the wealth. By World War I hatred of communists, anarchists, and agitators gripped a large part of the people, a hatred duly fanned by the media. The message was clear —strike out against the system and you will be smashed; come begging as a penitent, and you'll get a handout. Even more loudly trumpeted were doctrines of White supremacy, expressed in the popular writings of the geographer Ellsworth Huntington, who ranked the races from Northwest Europeans at the top to Africans at the bottom. The crudities of America's racist empire capitalism were to give way to more subtle methods in the ensuing decades of the twentieth century—the empire became the "free world"; radicals, like the militant labor unions, were welcomed into the system if they decided to play the game laid out for them; White supremacy gave way to Civil Rights which allowed our American *assimilados* to hold positions here and there in the system. Only ten years ago the rulers of America were in a state of euphoria believing that the empire at home and abroad was assured forever more.

Americans used to think of America as God's country. But if God gave it the power, wealth, and glory of empire, God has also not denied it the honor of Revolution. The American Revolution began in 1776 and has not yet ended.

When, a decade ago or so, America's rulers felt confident that they could incorporate the Third World into their empire, they found themselves facing an upsurge from the Third World within the national boundaries of the United States. That upsurge was led by the Black people. Black people had been forcibly brought to America as slaves for a feudal agriculture. The great majority of them remained as slaves to that same agriculture well into the twentieth century despite their legal emancipation. As that Southern agriculture crumbled before the onslaught of a more efficient and modern Western agriculture, Black people spread to all parts of America. If American capitalism had remained as dynamic as it was in the nineteenth century, the Black people would have been absorbed into the ever expanding industrial labor force. But as the empire grew,

America's capitalism showed growing signs of obesity and stagnation. It began to prefer importing consumer goods from abroad rather than producing them at home and so creating new forms of productive employment. Industry required ever greater skills, thus closing their doors to the poor. Unions, fearing automation, warded off the poor; their predominately White members often developed a paranoiac racism. Black people and other Third World poor poured into ghettos with no exit, subsisting in poverty and degradation like the peasants of inland China amongst whom the Chinese Revolution arose. The response of America's rulers, epitomized by Lyndon Baines Johnson's Great Society, was to offer them "bread and circuses"—welfare, menial employment, Black faces on TV and in the movies, and at the same time to skim off the cream of their *assimilado* elites. If it worked in the outer Third World, why should it not work in the inner Third World? And if there was resistance, just as in Vietnam, a bit of force could be applied to rid the peaceful peasants of the "scavengers of the modernization process."

Just as a great revolutionary process has begun in the outer Third World, so one has begun in the inner Third World of America. That process unites within itself all the elements that flowed out of the original eighteenth-century revolutions and those added by subsequent revolutions. The people of our inner Third World revolution want power— "not power over people, but the power to control our own destiny," in the words of Huey P. Newton. The people of our inner Third World Revolution want work, education, and the basis of a good life which capitalism gives its rulers and class allies. The people of the inner Third World Revolution want the liberty, equality, and fraternity which can only come about by finally doing away with the class divisions that hold fast in this country.

In this revolutionary process there has emerged the Black Panther Party, originally a political weapon of self-defense by Black people, but now a growing party with a vision reaching out to the entire world and a practice aiming deep into the communities of Black people. The context of the revolutionary movement within which the Black Panther Party grows is similar to that of other movements, notably the Chinese. As in China during the 1920's and 1930's, there are now the nationalist revolutionaries who want power, identity, and respect for their own race. There are also the "endorsed spokesmen," who while often vehement in language believe they can make personal gains by extorting concessions from the national and class oppressors. There are the "implacables" who desire to break the slave-master's oppressive power by any means necessary.

In China during the latter 1930's, the nationalists soon exhausted their energies, the endorsed spokesmen went over to the Japanese enemy, and the implacables were killed off leaving only the memory of their fortitude. Huey P. Newton speaks of "the three points of a triangle of death" which the oppressor, the "endorsed spokesmen," and the "implacables" form. The lesson of the Chinese Revolution shows that it was the Communist Party which evolved a revolutionary vision for all mankind, which developed a practice which went deep into the villages, and which kept on fighting external and internal oppressors while always committed to survival. This was the party led by Mao Tse-tung that carried on the revolution for the liberation of China. The Black Panther Party being led by Huey P. Newton is now developing along similar lines with vision, practice, and struggle. Representative of this development is the change in Newton's title: he is no longer the Minister of Defense, but the Servant of the People.

The vision of the Black Panther Party is expressed in the first part of this book, and the core of the vision is Revolutionary Intercommunalism. Revolutionary Intercommunalism is an idea which emerges out of a fundamental contradiction: that America is not a nation but an empire which directly or indirectly spans the globe, that its real units are communities which are ever more visible as one goes down into the poor Third World strata of America, and that that empire and community stand in dialectical contradiction and confrontation with each other. While peoples legitimately fight for nationhood throughout the world, in a fundamental sense, nations cannot really exist for long because all nations fall somewhere on a scale from liberated to non-liberated territories. As Newton says of Cuba, The People's Republic of China, North Korea, North Vietnam, The Provisional Revolutionary Government of South Vietnam, "they represent the people's liberated territory."

The American empire is everywhere, even in China, a fact dramatically demonstrated by Nixon's visit. But the struggle against that empire takes form in the growth of communities able to produce, educate, and defend themselves. And the struggle expresses the revolutionary process when these communities forge linkages among themselves within nations and reach across national boundaries to different national communities. The Third World in America can never become a part of the American nation because there is no nation. To become a part means joining the empire which for most Third World people means to do so in a menial capacity. Third World people live in communities not by choice but because they are forced to remain in demarcated ghettos. Millions of White Americans live not in communities but as atomized individuals and in households. Nothing is more natural to man than to live in a community, but nothing is so abhorrent to the doctrines of "freedom" of the empire than that man should live in a community which escapes the manipulation of the rulers. The "villages" of the world have much to teach its "cities." "We cannot make our stand as nationalists," for the closer one is to the center of the empire, the more illusory the idea of nationhood is for any people. "We cannot even make our stand as internationalists," for an aggregate of citizens of the world is little more than an aggregate of bourgeois individualists. "We must place our hopes on the philosophy of intercommunalism"—only those who are by, through, and from a community can serve the great family of humankind. To go out, one must go deep. But to go deep, one must also go out.

"It is our belief," says Newton, "that the Black people in America are the only people who can free the world, loosen the yoke of colonialism, and destroy the war machine." The revolutionary process shows that people will be liberated, that the liberation of the outer and inner Third World is the key element in that process, and the Black people of the empire's heartland are at the center of revolutionary action.

The practice of the Black Panther Party is expressed in the second part of this book. The Party is a revolutionary vehicle made up of three elements: a small but dedicated cadre of workers who are willing to devote their full time to the goals of the organization; an organized structure through which the cadre can function; and revolutionary concepts which define and interpret phenomena, and establish the goals toward which the political vehicle will work. This is one side of practice. Its other indispensable side is "the building of a community structure," the development of basic survival programs for the people amongst whom the Party lives and serves and derives nourishment. The practice of the Black Panther Party is much like the building of base areas which the Chinese Communists engaged in during the 1930's. Building base areas sounds romantic with dashing guerrillas going out on forays against Japanese and Kuomintang oppressors. In reality it involved hard work day after day: planting crops, educating adults and children, organizing disaster relief, tending the sick, talking with the people. But when the oppressor came into the village, all united in defense of their achievements. And when the time came to unite with distant villages and party units for the attainment of larger goals, the cadres and many of the people went forth. They now understood that the large goals and the small goals were inextricably bound together. But the cadres also understood that the large goals were meaningless unless the smaller goals could be attained. As Newton says, ". . . they have to see first some basic accomplishments in order to realize that major successes are possible."

The writings of Huey Newton also makes clear that above all, the cadres and the people must know things as they are, and not just find pleasure in celestial or revolutionary rhetoric. "We always emphasized a concrete analysis of conditions." Even when the Black Panther Party was first founded, "its dreamers were armed with an ideology which provided a systematic method of analysis of how best to meet those needs." But concrete analysis must never be of the type done by the sociological snooper who coldly collects and assorts his data. "We are interested in everything the people are interested in." All great revolutions, despite what bourgeois theorists with their elitist notions have written, have always succeeded where the leaders and cadres were the "vehicles" of the people, where they were able to translate into organized and effective action the things the people wanted.

The struggle of the Black Panther Party is expressed in the third and last part of the book. The Servant of the People writes of comrades who have died and who were or are in prison. That struggle against oppression means suffering and imprisonment, and death is a lesson that one has to learn again and again. That empire means suffering, imprisonment, and death for other peoples is something many Americans have learned. That this empire will eventually bring its horrors home to America is something we have yet to learn. But struggle also has a dialectic of its own, for it produces that most wonderful of human bonds—comradeship. No one has understood the struggle of the Vietnamese people unless he or she realizes that its basis is the extraordinary comradeship that has arisen in a quarter century of struggle. Americans seem not to understand comradeship because they no longer know what friendship means. A friend is anyone you happen to meet. Those who died like Jonathan Jackson and William Christmas may appear to many sympathetic Americans as tragic victims of prison oppression. These same Americans also think of the Vietnamese as "victims," but anyone who has been to North Vietnam soon loses that notion. Nor were those who died in this country for Black liberation "victims"; they were comrades. As the struggle deepens and spreads in America, so will the bonds of comradeship.

The Black Panther Party may now have come through its own Long March, and a period of building, survival, and protracted struggle begun. If there be similarities to China's Long March, they are not due to conscious imitation, but manifestations of a larger and longer revolutionary process which does not spring out of the alert minds of some individuals, but from the people.

Franz Schurmann
San Francisco
February 29, 1972

I

The Party

*The Black Panther
Party is an ox
for the people.*

1. We want freedom. We want power to determine the destiny of our Black Community.

We believe that black people will not be free until we are able to determine our destiny.

2. We want full employment for our people.

We believe that the federal government is responsible and obligated to give every man employment or a guaranteed income. We believe that if the White American businessmen will not give full employment, then the means of production should be taken from the businessmen and placed in the community so that the people of the community can organize and employ all of its people and give a high standard of living.

3. We want an end to the robbery by the CAPITALIST of our Black Community.

We believe that this racist government has robbed us and now we are demanding the overdue debt of forty acres and two mules. Forty acres and two mules was promised 100 years ago as restitution for slave labor and mass murder of Black people. We will accept the payment in currency which will be distributed to our many communities. The Germans are now aiding the Jews in Israel for the genocide of the Jewish people. The Germans murdered six million Jews. The American racist has taken part in the slaughter of over fifty million Black people; therefore, we feel that this is a modest demand that we make.

4. We want decent housing fit for shelter of human beings.

We believe that if the White landlords will not give decent housing to our Black community, then the housing and the land should be made into cooperatives so that our community, with government aid, can build and make decent housing for its people.

5. We want education for our people that exposes the true nature of this decadent American society. We want education that teaches us our true history and our role in the present-day society.

We believe in an educational system that will give to our people a knowledge of self. If a man does not have knowledge of himself and his position in society and the world, then he has little chance to relate to anything else.

6. We want all Black men to be exempt from military service.

We believe that Black people should not be forced to fight in the military service to defend a racist government that does not protect us. We will not fight and kill other people of color in the world who, like Black people, are being victimized by the White racist government of America. We will protect ourselves from the force and violence of the racist police and the racist military, by whatever means necessary.

7. We want an immediate end to POLICE BRUTALITY and MURDER of Black people.

We believe we can end police brutality in our Black community by organizing Black self-defense groups that are dedicated to defending our Black community from racist police oppression and brutality. The second Amendment to the Constitution of the United States gives a right to bear arms. We therefore believe that all Black people should arm themselves for self-defense.

8. We want freedom for all Black men held in federal, state, county and city prisons and jails.

We believe that all Black people should be released from the many jails and prisons because they have not received a fair and impartial trial.

9. We want all Black People when brought to trial to be tried in court by a jury of their peer group or people from their Black communities, as defined by the Constitution of the United States.

We believe that the courts should follow the United States Constitution so that Black people will receive fair trials. The 14th Amendment of the U.S. Constitution gives a man a right to be tried by his peer group. A peer is a person from a similar economic, social, religious, geographical, environmental, historical and racial background. To do this the court will be forced to select a jury from the Black community from which the Black defendant came. We have been, and are being tried by all-White juries that have no understanding of the "average reasoning man" of the Black community.

10. We want land, bread, housing, education, clothing, justice and peace.

When, in the course of human events, it becomes necessary for one people to dissolve the political bands which have connected them with another, and to assume, among the powers of the earth, the separate and equal station to which the laws of nature and nature's God entitle them, a decent respect to the opinions of mankind requires that they should declare the causes which impel them to the separation.

We hold these truths to be self-evident, that all men are

created equal; that they are endowed by their Creator with certain unalienable rights; that among these are life, liberty, and the pursuit of happiness. **That, to secure these rights, governments are instituted among men, deriving their just powers from the consent of the governed; that, whenever any form of government becomes destructive of these ends, it is the right of the people to alter or to abolish it, and to institute a new government, laying its foundation on such principles, and organizing its powers in such form, as to them shall seem most likely to effect their safety and happiness.** Prudence, indeed, will dictate that governments long established should not be changed for light and transient causes; and, accordingly, all experience hath shown that mankind are more disposed to suffer, while evils are sufferable, than to right themselves by abolishing the forms to which they are accustomed. **But, when a long train of abuses and usurpations, pursuing invariably the same object, evinces a design to reduce them under absolute despotism, it is their right, it is their duty, to throw off such government, and to provide new guards for their future security.**

*Executive Mandate No. 1: May 2, 1967**

The Black Panther Party for Self-Defense calls upon the American people in general, and Black people in particular, to take careful note of the racist California Legislature now considering legislation aimed at keeping Black people disarmed and powerless while racist police agencies throughout the country intensify the terror, brutality, murder, and repression of Black people.

At the same time that the American Government is waging a racist war of genocide in Vietnam the concentration camps in which Japanese-Americans were interned during World War II are being renovated and expanded. Since America has historically reserved its most barbaric treatment for non-White people, we are forced to conclude that these concentration camps are being prepared for Black people who are determined to gain their freedom by any means necessary. The enslavement of Black people at the very founding of this country, the genocide practiced on the American Indians and the confinement of the survivors on reservations, the savage lynching of thousands of Black men and women, the dropping of atomic bombs on Hiroshima and Nagasaki, and now the cowardly massacre in Vietnam all testify to the fact that toward people of color the racist power structure of America has but one policy: repression, genocide, terror, and the big stick.

* Delivered at Sacramento, California, State Capitol Building. This and the two "Mandates" that follow were public statements made by Huey P. Newton as Minister of Defense of the Black Panther Party.

Black people have begged, prayed, petitioned and demonstrated, among other things, to get the racist power structure of America to right the wrongs which have historically been perpetrated against Black people. All of these efforts have been answered by more repression, deceit, and hypocrisy. As the aggression of the racist American Government escalates in Vietnam, the police agencies of America escalate the repression of Black people throughout the ghettos of America. Vicious police dogs, cattle prods, and increased patrols have become familiar sights in Black communities. City Hall turns a deaf ear to the pleas of Black people for relief from this increasing terror.

The Black Panther Party for Self-Defense believes that the time has come for Black people to arm themselves against this terror before it is too late. The pending Mulford Act* brings the hour of doom one step nearer. A people who have suffered so much for so long at the hands of a racist society must draw the line somewhere. We believe that the Black communities of America must rise up as one man to halt the progression of a trend that leads inevitably to their total destruction.

---

* A bill introduced into the California State Legislature in early 1967 by State Assemblyman Mulford. This bill resulted in changing crucial gun laws in the state, and was primarily introduced to thwart the just activity of the Black Panther Party. It was subsequent to the Black Panther Party's legal, armed defense patrols of local police that this bill was quickly pushed through the legislature. During the time of legislative debate around the bill (May of 1967), members of the Black Panther Party went to the State Capitol Building in Sacramento in an armed protest demonstration, declaring, in what became Executive Mandate Number One of the Black Panther Party, that Black people as an oppressed people had the right under the U.S. Constitution to bear arms in their defense. Passed in July of 1967, the Mulford Bill outlawed (in California, under Penal Codes 12031 and 171.C) carrying loaded firearms on one's person or in vehicles, and an ordinary citizen's having a loaded firearm in or near the State Capitol Building or any other state or government building, restricted area, etc.

So Let This Be Heard . . .
    Brother Stokely Carmichael:
Because you have distinguished yourself in the struggle for
the total liberation of Black people from oppression in
racist White America;

Because you have acted courageously and shown great
fortitude under the most adverse circumstances;

Because you have proven yourself a true revolutionary
guided by a great feeling of love for our people;

Because you have set such a fine example, in the tradition
of Brother Malcolm, of dedicating your entire life to the
struggle of Black Liberation, inspiring our youth and providing a model for others to emulate;

Because you have refused to serve in the oppressor's racist
mercenary, aggressive war machine, showing that you
know who your true friends and enemies are;

Because your new endeavor to organize and liberate the
Crown Colony of Washington, D.C., will inevitably force
you to confront, deal with, and conquer the racist Washington Police Department, which functions as the protector of
the racist dog power structure that occupies the Black
Community in the same manner and for the same reasons

that the racist U.S. Armed Forces occupy South Vietnam; You are hereby drafted into the Black Panther Party for Self-Defense, invested with the rank of Field Marshal, delegated the following authority, power, and responsibility:

To establish revolutionary law, order and justice in the territory lying between the Continental Divide East to the Atlantic Ocean; North of the Mason-Dixon Line to the Canadian Border; South of the Mason-Dixon Line to the Gulf of Mexico.

. . . So Let It Be Done.

Executive Mandate No. 3:
March 1, 1968

So Let This Be Heard:

Because of the St. Valentine's Day Massacre of February 14, 1929, in which outlaws donned the uniforms of policemen, posed as such, and thereby gained entrance to locked doors controlled by rival outlaws with whom they were contending for control of the bootlegging industry in Chicago; and because these gangsters, gaining entry through their disguise as policemen, proceeded to exterminate their rivals with machine-gun fire, we believe that prudence would dictate that one should be alert when opening one's door to strangers, late at night, in the wee hours of the morning—even when these strangers wear the uniform of policemen. History teaches us that a man in the uniform may or may not be a policeman authorized to enter the homes of the people.

AND

Taking notice of the fact that on January 16, 1968, at 3:30 A.M., members of the San Francisco Police Department kicked down the door, made an illegal entry and search of the home of Eldridge Cleaver, Minister of Information. These Pigs were not invited in, had no search warrant, no arrest warrant, and were therefore not authorized to enter. Permission for them to enter was explicitly denied by the Minister of Information. Present were Sister Kathleen Cleaver, our Communications Secretary and wife to our Minister of Information, and Brother Emory Douglas, our Revolutionary Artist.

Taking further notice of the fact that on February 25, 1968, several uniformed gestapos of the Berkeley Pig Department, accompanied by several other White men in plain clothes, bearing an assortment of shotguns, rifles, and service revolvers, made a forceful, unlawful entry and search of the home of Bobby Seale, Chairman of our Party, and his wife, Sister Artie Seale. These Pigs had no warrant either to search or to arrest. When asked by Chairman Bobby to produce a warrant they arrogantly stated that they did not need one. They had no authority to enter— what they did have was the power of the gun.

On the basis of these two incidents we are convinced that the situation is critical. Our organization has received serious threats from certain racist elements of White America, including the Oakland, Berkeley, and San Francisco Pig Departments. Threats to take our lives, to exterminate us. We cannot determine when any of these elements or a combination of them may move to implement these threats. We must be alert to the danger at all times. We will not fall victim to another St. Valentine's Day Massacre. Therefore, those who approach our doors in the manner of outlaws; who seek to enter our homes illegally, unlawfully and in a rowdy fashion; those who kick our doors down with no authority and seek to ransack our homes in violation of our HUMAN RIGHTS will henceforth be treated as outlaws, as gangsters, as evil-doers. We have no way of determining that a man in a uniform involved in a forced outlaw entry into our home is in fact a guardian of the Law. He is acting like a law-breaker and we must make an appropriate response.

We draw the line at the threshold of our doors. It is therefore mandated as a general order to all members of the Black Panther Party for Self-Defense that all members must acquire the technical equipment to defend their homes and their dependents and shall do so. Any member of the Party having such technical equipment who fails to defend his threshold shall be expelled from the Party for Life.

. . . So Let This Be Done.

The Correct Handling of a Revolution:
July 20, 1967*

The Black masses are handling the resistance incorrectly. When the brothers in East Oakland, having learned their resistance fighting from Watts, amassed the people in the streets, threw bricks and Molotov cocktails to destroy property and create disruption, they were herded into a small area by the gestapo police and immediately contained by the brutal violence of the oppressor's storm troops. Although this manner of resistance is sporadic, short-lived, and costly, it has been transmitted across the country to all the ghettos of the Black nation.

The identity of the first man who threw a Molotov cocktail is not known by the masses, yet they respect and imitate his action. In the same way, the actions of the party will be imitated by the people—if the people respect these activities.

The primary job of the party is to provide leadership for the people. It must teach by words and action the correct strategic methods of prolonged resistance. When the people learn that it is no longer advantageous for them to resist by going into the streets in large numbers, and when they see the advantage in the activities of the guerrilla warfare method, they will quickly follow this example.

But first, they must respect the party which is transmitting this message. When the vanguard group destroys the machinery of the oppressor by dealing with him in small

* From "In Defense of Self-Defense," Huey Newton's column in the Black Panther newspaper.

groups of three and four, and then escapes the might of the oppressor, the masses will be impressed and more likely to adhere to this correct strategy. When the masses hear that a gestapo policeman has been executed while sipping coffee at a counter, and the revolutionary executioners fled without being traced, the masses will see the validity of this kind of resistance. It is not necessary to organize thirty million Black people in primary groups of two's and three's, but it is important for the party to show the people how to stage a revolution.

There are three ways one can learn: through study, observation, and experience. Since the Black community is composed basically of activists, observation of or participation in activity are the principle ways the community learns. To learn by studying is good, but to learn by experience is better. Because the Black community is not a reading community it is very important that the vanguard group be essentially activists. Without this knowledge of the Black community a Black revolution in racist America is impossible.

The main function of the party is to awaken the people and teach them the strategic method of resisting a power structure which is prepared not only to combat with massive brutality the people's resistance but to annihilate totally the Black population. If it is learned by the power structure that Black people have "X" number of guns in their possession, that information will not stimulate the power structure to prepare itself with guns; it is already prepared.

The end result of this revolutionary education will be positive for Black people in their resistance, and negative for the power structure in its oppression because the party always exemplifies revolutionary defiance. If the party does not make the people aware of the tools and methods of liberation, there will be no means by which the people can mobilize.

The relationship between the vanguard party and the masses is a secondary relationship. The relationship among the members of the vanguard party is a primary relationship. If the party machinery is to be effective it is important that the members of the party group maintain a face-to-face relationship with each other. It is impossible to put together functional party machinery or programs without this direct relationship. To minimize the danger of Uncle Tom informers and opportunists the members of the vanguard group should be tested revolutionaries.

The main purpose of the vanguard group should be to raise the consciousness of the masses through educational programs and other activities. The sleeping masses must be bombarded with the correct approach to struggle and the party must use all means available to get this information across to the masses. In order to do so the masses must know that the party exists. A vanguard party is never underground in the beginning of its existence; that would limit its effectiveness and educational goals. How can you teach people if the people do not know and respect you? The party must exist aboveground as long as the dog power structure will allow, and, hopefully, when the party is forced to go underground, the party's message will already have been put across to the people. The vanguard party's activities on the surface will necessarily be short-lived. Thus the party must make a tremendous impact upon the people before it is driven into secrecy. By that time the people will know the party exists and will seek further information about its activities when it is driven underground.

Many would-be revolutionaries work under the fallacious notion that the vanguard party should be a secret organization which the power structure knows nothing about, and that the masses know nothing about except for occasional letters that come to their homes by night. Underground parties cannot distribute leaflets announcing an underground meeting. Such contradictions and inconsistencies are not recognized by these so-called revolutionaries. They are, in fact, afraid of the very danger that they are asking the people to confront. These so-called revolutionaries want the people to say what they themselves are afraid to say, to do what they themselves are afraid to do. That kind of revolutionary is a coward and a hypocrite. A true revolutionary realizes that if he is sincere death is imminent. The things he is saying and doing are extremely dangerous. Without this realization it is pointless to proceed as a revolutionary.

If these imposters would investigate the history of revolution they would see that the vanguard group always starts out aboveground and is driven underground by the aggressor. The Cuban Revolution is an example: when Fidel Castro started to resist the butcher Batista and the American running dogs, he began by speaking publicly on the University of Havana campus. He was later driven to the hills. His impact upon the dispossessed people of Cuba was tremendous and his teachings were received with much respect. When he went into hiding, the Cuban people searched him out, going to the hills to find him and his band of twelve.

Castro handled the revolutionary struggle correctly, and if the Chinese Revolution is investigated it will be seen that the Communist Party operated quite openly in order to muster support from the masses. There are many more examples of successful revolutionary struggle from which one can learn the correct approach: the revolution in Kenya, the Algerian Revolution discussed in Fanon's *The Wretched of the Earth,* the Russian Revolution, the works of Chairman Mao Tse-tung, and a host of others.

Millions and millions of oppressed people may not know members of the vanguard party personally but they will learn of its activities and its proper strategy for liberation through an indirect acquaintance provided by the mass media. But it is not enough to rely on the media of the power structure; it is of prime importance that the vanguard party develop its own communications organ, such as a newspaper, and at the same time provide strategic revolutionary art, and destruction of the oppressor's machinery. For example in Watts the economy and property of the oppressor was destroyed to such an extent that no matter how the oppressor tried in his press to whitewash the activities of the Black brothers, the real nature and cause of the activity was communicated to every Black community. And no matter how the oppressor tried in his own media to distort and confuse the message of Brother Stokely Carmichael, Black people all over the country understood it perfectly and welcomed it.

The Black Panther Party for Self-Defense teaches that, in the final analysis the guns, hand grenades, bazookas, and other equipment necessary for defense must be supplied by the power structure. As exemplified by the Vietcong, these weapons must be taken from the oppressor. Therefore, the greater the military preparation on the part of the oppressor, the greater the availability of weapons for the Black community. It is believed by some hypocrites that when the people are taught by the vanguard group to prepare for resistance, this only brings "the man" down on them with increasing violence and brutality; but the fact is that when the man becomes more oppressive he only heightens revolutionary fervor. So if things get worse for oppressed people they will feel the need for revolution and resistance. The people make revolution; the oppressors, by their brutal actions, cause resistance by the people. The vanguard party only teaches the correct methods of resistance.

The complaint of the hypocrites that the Black Panther Party for Self-Defense is exposing the people to deeper suffering is an incorrect observation. By their rebellions in the Black communities across the country the people have proved that they will not tolerate any more oppression by the racist dog police. They are looking now for guidance to extend and strengthen their resistance struggle. The vanguard party must exemplify the characteristics that make them worthy of leadership.

Power to the people, brothers and sisters. I would like to thank you for my presence here tonight because you are responsible for it. I would be in a maximum-security penitentiary if it were not for the power of the people.

I would like to petition you to do the same for Bobby Seale, our Chairman, for Ericka Huggins, for Angela Davis, for the New York 21 and the Soledad Brothers. For all political prisoners and prisoners of war. On the 28th and 29th of November we will have a People's Revolutionary Constitutional convention in Washington, D.C. We cannot have that convention if the people do not come. After all, the people are the makers of world history and responsible for everything. How can we have a convention if we have no people? Some believe a people's convention is possible without the people being there. As I recall, that was the case in 1777.

Tonight, I would like to outline for you the Black Panther Party's program and explain how we arrived at our ideological position and why we feel it necessary to institute a Ten-Point Program. A Ten-Point Program is not revolutionary in itself, nor is it reformist. *It is a survival program.* We, the people, are threatened with genocide because racism and fascism are rampant in this country and throughout the world. And the ruling circle in North America is responsible. We intend to change all of that, and in order to change it, there must be a total transformation. But until we can achieve that total transformation, we must exist. In order to exist, we must survive; therefore, we need a survival kit: the Ten-Point Program. It is necessary for our children to grow up healthy with functional and creative minds. They cannot do this if they do not get the correct nutrition. That is why we have a breakfast program for children. We also have community health programs. We have a busing program. We call it "The Bus for Relatives and Parents of Prisoners." We realize that the fascist regime that operates the prisons throughout America would like to do their treachery in the dark. But if we get the relatives, parents, and friends to the prisons they can expose the treachery of the fascists. This too is a survival program.

We must not regard our survival programs as an answer to the whole problem of oppression. We don't even claim it to be a revolutionary program. Revolutions are made of sterner stuff. We do say that if the people are not here revolution cannot be achieved, for the people and only the people make revolutions.

The theme of our Revolutionary People's Constitutional Convention is "Survival Through Service to the People." At our convention we will present our total survival program. It is a program that works very much like the first-aid kit that is used when a plane falls and you find yourself in the middle of the sea on a rubber raft. You need a few things to last until you can get to the shore, until you can get to that oasis where you can be happy and healthy. If you do not have the things necessary to get you to that shore, then you will probably not exist. At this time the ruling circle threatens us to the extent that we are afraid that we might not exist to see the next day or see the revolution. The Black Panther Party will not accept the total destruction of the people. As a matter of fact, we have drawn a line of demarcation and we will no longer tolerate fascism, aggression, brutality, and murder of any kind. We will not sit around and allow ourselves to be murdered. Each person has an obligation to preserve himself. If he does not preserve himself then I accuse him of suicide: reactionary suicide because reactionary conditions will have caused his death. If we do nothing we are accepting the situation and allowing ourselves to die. We will not accept that. If the alternatives are very narrow we still will not sit around, we will not die the death of the Jews in Germany. We would rather die the death of the Jews in Warsaw!

Where there is courage, where there is self-respect and dignity, there is a possibility that we can change the conditions and win. This is called *revolutionary enthusiasm* and it is the kind of struggle that is needed in order to guarantee a victory. If we must die, then we will die the death of a revolutionary suicide that says, "If I am put down, if I am driven out, I refuse to be swept out with a broom. I would much rather be driven out with a stick because if I am swept out with the broom it will humiliate me and I will lose my self-respect. But if I am driven out with the stick, then, at least, I can claim the dignity of a man and die the death of a man rather than the death of a dog." Of course, our real desire is to live, but we will not be cowed, we will not be intimidated.

I would like to explain to you the method that the Black Panther Party used to arrive at our ideological position, and more than that, I would like to give to you a framework or a process of thinking that might help us solve the problems and the contradictions that exist today. Before we approach the problem we must get a clear picture of what is really going on; a clear image divorced from the attitudes and emotions that we usually project into a situation. We must be as objective as possible without accepting dogma, letting the facts speak for themselves. But we will not remain totally objective; we will become subjective in the application of the knowledge received from the external world. We will use the scientific method to acquire this knowledge, but we will openly acknowledge our ultimate subjectivity. Once we apply knowledge in order to *will* a certain outcome our objectivity ends and our subjectivity begins. We call this integrating theory with practice, and this is what the Black Panther Party is all about.

In order to understand a group of forces operating at the same time, science developed what is called the scientific method. One of the characteristics or properties of this method is disinterest. Not *un*interest, but disinterest: no special interest in the outcome. In other words, the scientist does not promote an outcome, he just collects the facts. Nevertheless, in acquiring his facts he must begin with a basic premise. Most basic premises stem from a set of assumptions because it is very difficult to test a first premise without these assumptions. After an agreement is reached on certain assumptions, an intelligent argument can follow, for then logic and consistency are all that is required to reach a valid conclusion.

Tonight I ask you to assume that an external world exists. An external world that exists independently of us. The second assumption I would like for you to make is that things are in a constant state of change, transformation, or flux. With agreement on these two assumptions we can go on with our discussion.

The scientific method relies heavily on empiricism. But the problem with empiricism is that it tells you very little about the future; it tells you only about the past, about information which you have already discovered through observation and experience. It always refers to past experience.

Long after the rules of empirical knowledge had been ascertained, a man by the name of Karl Marx integrated these rules with a theory developed by Immanuel Kant called rationale. Kant called his process of reasoning pure reason because it did not depend on the external world. Instead it only depended on consistency in manipulating symbols in order to come up with a conclusion based upon reason. For example, in this sentence "If the sky is above my head when I turn my head upwards, I will see the sky" there is nothing wrong with the conclusion. As a matter of fact, it is accurate. But I haven't said anything about the existence of the sky. I said "if." With rationale we are not dependent upon the external world. With empiricism we can tell very little about the future. So what will we do? What Marx did. In order to understand what was happening in the world Marx found it necessary to integrate rationale with empiricism. He called his concept dialectical materialism. If, like Marx, we integrate these two concepts or these two ways of thinking, not only are we in touch with the world outside us but we can also explain the constant state of transformation. Therefore, we can also make some predictions about the outcome of certain social phenomena that is not only in constant change but also in conflict.

Marx, as a social scientist, criticized other social scientists for attempting to explain phenomena, or one phenomenon, by taking it out of its environment, isolating it, putting it into a category, and not acknowledging the fact that once it was taken out of its environment the phenomenon was transformed. For example, if in a discipline such as sociology we study the activity of groups—how they hold together and why they fall apart—without understanding everything else related to that group, we may arrive at a false conclusion about the nature of the group. What Marx attempted to do was to develop a way of thinking that would explain phenomena realistically.

In the physical world, when forces collide they are transformed. When atoms collide, in physics, they divide into electrons, protons, and neutrons, if I remember correctly. What happened to the atom? It was transformed. In the social world a similar thing happens. We can apply the same principle. When two cultures collide a process or condition occurs which the sociologists call acculturation: the modification of cultures as a result of their contact with each other. Marx called the collision of social forces or classes a contradiction. In the physical world, when forces collide we sometimes call it just that—a collision. For example, when two cars meet head on, trying to occupy the same space at the same time, both are transformed. Sometimes other things happen. Had those two cars been turned back to back and sped off in opposite directions they would not be a contradiction; they would be contrary, covering different spaces at different times. Sometimes when people meet they argue and misunderstand each other because they think they are having a contradiction when they are only being contrary. For example, I can say the wall is ten feet tall and you can say the wall is red, and we can argue all day thinking we are having a contradiction when actually we are only being contrary. When people argue, when one offers a thesis and the other offers an anti-thesis, we say there is a contradiction and hope that if we argue long enough, provided that we agree on one premise, we can have some kind of synthesis. Tonight I hope I can have some form of agreement or synthesis with those who have criticized the Black Panther Party.

I think that the mistake is either that some people have taken the apparent as the actual fact in spite of their claims of scholarly research and following the discipline of dialectical materialism. They fail to search deeper, as the scientist is required to do, to get beyond the apparent and come up with the more significant. Let me explain how this relates to the Black Panther Party. The Black Panther Party is a Marxist-Leninist party because we follow the dialectical method and we also integrate theory with practice. We are not mechanical Marxists and we are not historical materialists. Some people think they are Marxists when actually they are following the thoughts of Hegel. Some people think they are Marxist-Leninists but they refuse to be creative, and are, therefore, tied to the past. They are tied to a rhetoric that does not apply to the present set of conditions.

They are tied to a set of thoughts that approaches dogma—what we call flunkyism.

Marx attempted to set up a framework which could be applied to a number of conditions. And in applying this framework we cannot be afraid of the outcome because things change and we must be willing to acknowledge that change because we are objective. If we are using the method of dialectical materialism we don't expect to find anything the same even one minute later because "one minute later" is history. If things are in a constant state of change, we cannot expect them to be the same. Words used to describe old phenomena may be useless to describe the new. And if we use the old words to describe new events we run the risk of confusing people and misleading them into thinking that things are static.

In 1917 an event occurred in the Soviet Union that was called a revolution. Two classes had a contradiction and the whole country was transformed. In this country, 1970, the Black Panther Party issued a document. Our Minister of Information, Eldridge Cleaver, who now is in Algeria, wrote a pamphlet called "On the Ideology of the Black Panther Party." In that work Eldridge Cleaver stated that neither the proletarians nor the industrial workers carry the potentialities for revolution in this country at this time. He claimed that the left wing of the proletarians, the lumpen-proletarians, have that revolutionary potential, and in fact, acting as the vanguard, they would carry the people of the world to the final climax of the transformation of society. It has been stated by some people, by some parties, by some organizations, by the Progressive Labor Party, that revolution is impossible. How can the lumpenproletarians carry out a successful socialist transformation when they are only a minority? And in fact how can they do it when history shows that only the proletarians have carried out a successful social revolution? I agree that it is necessary for the people who carry out a social revolution to represent the popular majority's interests. It is necessary for this group to represent the broad masses of the people. We analyzed what happened in the Soviet Union in 1917. I also agree that the lumpenproletarians are the minority in this country. No disagreement. Have I contradicted myself? It only goes to show that what's apparent might not actually be a fact. What appears to be a contradiction may be only a paradox. Let's examine this apparent contradiction.

The Soviet Union, in 1917, was basically an agricultural society with a very large peasantry. A set of social conditions existing there at that time was responsible for the development of a small industrial base. The people who worked in this industrial base were called proletarians. Lenin, using Marx's theory, saw the trends. He was not a historical materialist, but a dialectical materialist, and therefore very interested in the ever-changing status of things. He saw that while the proletarians were a minority in 1917, they had the potential to carry out a revolution because their class was increasing and the peasantry was declining. That was one of the conditions. The proletarians were destined to be a popular force. They also had access to the properties necessary for carrying out a socialist revolution.

In this country the Black Panther Party, taking careful note of the dialectical method, taking careful note of the social trends and the ever-changing nature of things, sees that while the lumpenproletarians are the minority and the proletarians are the majority, technology is developing at such a rapid rate that automation will progress to cybernation, and cybernation probably to technocracy. As I came into town I saw MIT over the way. If the ruling circle remains in power it seems to me that capitalists will continue to develop their technological machinery because they are not interested in the people. Therefore, I expect from them the logic that they have always followed: to make as much money as possible, and pay the people as little as possible—until the people demand more, and finally demand their heads. If revolution does not occur almost immediately, and I say almost immediately because technology is making leaps (it made a leap all the way to the moon), and if the ruling circle remains in power the proletarian working class will definitely be on the decline because they will be unemployables and therefore swell the ranks of the lumpens, who are the present unemployables. Every worker is in jeopardy because of the ruling circle, which is why we say that the lumpenproletarians have the potential for revolution, will probably carry out the revolution, and in the near future will be the popular majority. Of course, I would not like to see more of my people unemployed or become unemployables, but being objective, because we're dialectical materialists, we must acknowledge the facts.

Marx outlined a rough process of the development of society. He said that society goes from a slave class to a feudalistic class structure to a capitalistic class structure to a socialistic class structure and finally to communism. Or in other words, from capitalist state to socialist state to non-state: communism. I think we can all agree that the slave class in the world has virtually been transformed into the wage slave. In other words, the slave class in the world no longer exists as a significant force, and if we agree to that we can agree that classes can be transformed literally out of existence. If this is so, if the slave class can disappear and become something else—or not disappear but just be transformed—and take on other characteristics, then it is also true that the proletarians or the industrial working class can possibly be transformed out of existence. Of course the people themselves would not disappear; they would only take on other attributes. The attribute that I am interested in is the fact that soon the ruling circle will not need the workers, and if the ruling circle is in control of the means of production the working class will become unemployables or lumpens. That is logical; that is dialectical. I think it would be wrong to say that only the slave class could disappear.

Marx was a very intelligent man. He was not a dogmatist. Once he said, "One thing I'm not, I'm not a Marxist." In those words, he was trying to tell the Progressive Labor Party and others not to accept the past as the present or the future, but to understand it and be able to predict what might happen in the future and therefore act in an intelligent way to bring about the revolution that we all want.

After taking those things into consideration we see that as time changes and the world is transformed we need some new definitions, for if we keep using the old terms people might think the old situation still exists. I would be amazed if the same conditions that existed in 1917 were still existing today.

You know Marx and Lenin were pretty lazy dudes when it came to working for somebody. They looked at toil, working for your necessities, as something of a curse. And Lenin's whole theory, after he put Marx's analysis into practice, was geared to get rid of the proletarians. In other words, when the proletarian class or the working class seized the means of production, they would plan their society in such a way as to be free from toil. As a matter of fact, Lenin saw a time in which man could stand in one place, push buttons and move mountains. It sounds to me as though he saw a proletarian working class transformed and in possession of a free block of time, to indulge in productive creativity, to think about developing their universe, so that they could have the happiness, the freedom and the pleasure that all men seek and value.

Today's capitalist has developed machinery to such a point that he can hire a group of specialized people called technocrats. In the near future he will certainly do more of this, and the technocrat will be too specialized to be identified as a proletarian. In fact that group of technocrats will be so vital we will have to do something to explain the presence of other people; we will have to come up with another definition and reason for existing.

But we must not confine our discussion to theory; we must have practical application of our theory to come up with anything worthwhile. In spite of the criticism that we have received from certain people, the Party has a practical application of its theories. Many of our activities provide the working class and the unemployed with a reason and a means for existing in the future. The people will not disappear—not with our survival programs they will not. They will still be around. The Black Panther Party says it is perfectly correct to organize the proletarians because after they are kicked out of the factory and are called unemployable or lumpen, they still want to live, and in order to live they have to eat. It is in the proletarian's own best interest to seize the machinery that he has made in order to produce in abundance, so he and his brethren can live. We will not wait until the proletarian becomes the lumpenproletarian to educate him. Today we must lift the consciousness of the people. The wind is rising and the rivers flowing, times are getting hard and we can't go home again. We can't go back to our mother's womb, nor can we go back to 1917.

The United States, or what I like to call North America, was transformed at the hands of the ruling circle from a nation to an empire. This caused a total change in the world, because no part of an interrelated thing can change and leave everything else the same. So when the United States, or North America, became an empire it changed the whole composition of the world. There were other nations in the world. But "empire" means that the ruling circle who lives in the empire (the imperialists) control other nations. Now some time ago there existed a phenomenon we called —well, I call—primitive empire. An example of that would be the Roman Empire because the Romans controlled all of what was thought to be the known world. In fact they did not know all of the world therefore some nations still existed independent of it. Now, probably all of the world is known. The United States as an empire necessarily controls the whole world either directly or indirectly.

If we understand dialectics we know that every determination brings about a limitation and every limitation brings about a determination. In other words, while one force may give rise to one thing it might crush other things, including itself. We might call this concept "the negation of the negation." So, while in 1917 the ruling circle created an industrial base and used the system of capitalism they were also creating the necessary conditions for socialism. They were doing this because in a socialist society it is necessary to have some centralization of the wealth, some equal distribution of the wealth, and some harmony among the people.

Now, I will give you roughly some characteristics that any people who call themselves a nation should have. These are economic independence, cultural determination, control of the political institutions, territorial integrity, and safety.

In 1966 we called our Party a Black Nationalist Party. We called ourselves Black Nationalists because we thought that nationhood was the answer. Shortly after that we decided that what was really needed was revolutionary nationalism, that is, nationalism plus socialism. After analyzing conditions a little more, we found that it was impractical and even contradictory. Therefore, we went to a higher level of consciousness. We saw that in order to be free we had to crush the ruling circle and therefore we had to unite with the peoples of the world. So we called ourselves Internationalists. We sought solidarity with the peoples of the world. We sought solidarity with what we thought were the nations of the world. But then what happened? We found that because everything is in a constant state of transformation, because of the development of technology, because of the development of the mass media, because of the fire power of the imperialist, and because of the fact that the United States is no longer a nation but an empire, nations could not exist, for they did not have the criteria for nationhood. Their self-determination, economic determination, and cultural determination has been transformed by the imperialists and the ruling circle. They were no longer nations. We found that in order to be Internationalists we had to be also Nationalists, or at least acknowledge nationhood. Internationalism, if I understand the word, means the interrelationship among a group of nations. But since no nation exists, and since the United States is in fact an empire, it is impossible for us to be Internationalists. These transformations and phenomena require us to call ourselves "intercommunalists" *because nations have been transformed into communities of the world.* The Black Panther Party now disclaims internationalism and supports intercommunalism.*

Marx and Lenin felt, with the information they had, that when the non-state finally came to be a reality, it would be caused or ushered in by the people and by communism. A strange thing happened. The ruling reactionary circle, through the consequence of being imperialists, transformed the world into what we call "Reactionary Intercommunalism." They laid siege upon all the communities of the world, dominating the institutions to such an extent that the people were not served by the institutions in their own land. The Black Panther Party would like to reverse that trend and lead the people of the world into the age of "Revolutionary Intercommunalism." This would be the time when the people seize the means of production and distribute the wealth and the technology in an egalitarian way to the many communities of the world.

We see very little difference in what happens to a community here in North America and what happens to a community in Vietnam. We see very little difference in what happens, even culturally, to a Chinese community in San Francisco and a Chinese community in Hong Kong. We see very little difference in what happens to a Black

* A term coined by Newton to describe the political philosophy of the Panthers and the alteration of economic, cultural, and political relationships in the world.

community in Harlem and a Black community in South Africa, a Black community in Angola and one in Mozambique. We see very little difference.

So, what has actually happened, is that the non-state has already been accomplished, but it is reactionary. A community by way of definition is a comprehensive collection of institutions which serve the people who live there. It differs from a nation because a community evolves around a greater structure that we usually call the state, and the state has certain control over the community if the administration represents the people or if the administration happens to be the people's commissar. It is not so at this time, so there's still something to be done. I mentioned earlier the "negation of the negation," I mentioned earlier the necessity for the redistribution of wealth. We think that it is very important to know that as things are in the world today socialism in the United States will never exist. Why? It will not exist because it cannot exist. It cannot at this time exist anyplace in the world. Socialism would require a socialist state, and if a state does not exist how could socialism exist? So how do we define certain progressive countries such as the People's Republic of China? How do we describe certain progressive countries, or communities as we call them, as the Democratic People's Republic of Korea? How do we define certain communities such as North Vietnam and the provisional government in the South? How do we explain these communities if in fact they too cannot claim nationhood? We say this: we say they represent the people's liberated territory. They represent a community liberated. But that community is not sufficient, it is not satisfied, just as the National Liberation Front is not satisfied with the liberated territory in the South. It is only the groundwork and preparation for the liberation of the world—seizing the wealth from the ruling circle, equal distribution and proportional representation in an intercommunal framework. This is what the Black Panther Party would like to achieve with the help of the power of the people, because without the people nothing can be achieved.

I stated that in the United States socialism would never exist. In order for a revolution to occur in the United States you would have to have a redistribution of wealth not on a national or an international level, but on an intercommunal level. Because how can we say that we have accomplished revolution if we redistribute the wealth just to the people here in North America when the ruling circle itself is guilty of *trespass de bonis asportatis*.* That is, they have taken away the goods of the people of the world, transported them to America and used them as their very own.

In 1917, when the revolution occurred, there could be a redistribution of wealth on a national level because nations existed. Now, if you talk in terms of planning an economy on a *world-wide* level, on an intercommunal level, you are saying something important: that the people have been ripped off very much like one country being ripped off. Simple reparation is not enough because the people have not only been robbed of their raw materials, but of the wealth accrued from the investment of those materials—an investment which has created the technological machine. The people of the world will have to have control—not a limited share of control for "X" amount of time, but total control forever.

In order to plan a real intercommunal economy we will have to acknowledge how the world is hooked up. We will also have to acknowledge that nations have not existed for some time. Some people will argue that nations still exist because of the cultural differences. By way of definition, just for practical argument, culture is a collection of learned patterns of behavior. Here in the United States Black people, Africans, were raped from the mother country, and consequently we have literally lost most of our

---

* Taking away the property of others and using it as one's own.

African values. Perhaps we still hold on to some surviving Africanisms, but by and large you can see the transformation which was achieved by time and the highly technological society whose tremendous mass media functions as an indoctrination center. The ruling circle has launched satellites in order to project a beam across the earth and indoctrinate the world, and while there might be some cultural differences, these differences are not qualitative but quantitative. In other words, if technology and the ruling circle go on as they are now the people of the world will be conditioned to adapt Western values. (I think Japan is a good example.) The differences between people are getting very small, but again that is in the interest of the ruling circle. I do not believe that history can be backtracked. If the world is really that interconnected then we have to acknowledge that and say that in order for the people to be free, they will have to control the institutions of their community, and have some form of representation in the technological center that they have produced. The United States, in order to correct its robbery of the world, will have to first return much of which it has stolen. I don't see how we can talk about socialism when the problem is world distribution. I think this is what Marx meant when he talked about the non-state.

I was at Alex Haley's house some time ago and he talked to me about his search for his past. He found it in Africa but when he returned there shortly afterward, he was in a state of panic. His village hadn't changed very much, but when he went there he saw an old man walking down the road, holding something that he cherished to his ear. It was a small transistor radio that was zeroed in on the British broadcasting network. What I'm trying to say is that mass media plus the development of transportation make it impossible for us to think of ourselves in terms of separate entities, as nations. Do you realize that it only took me approximately five hours to get from San Francisco to here?

It only takes ten hours to get from here to Vietnam. The ruling circle no longer even acknowledges wars; they call them "police actions." They call the riots of the Vietnamese people "domestic disturbance." What I am saying is that the ruling circle must realize and accept the consequences of what they have done. They know that there is only one world, but they are determined to follow the logic of their exploitation.

A short time ago in Detroit, the community was under siege, and now sixteen members of the Party are in prison. The local police laid siege on that community and that house, and they used the same weapons they use in Vietnam (as a matter of fact, two tanks rolled up). The same thing happens in Vietnam because the "police" are there also. The "police" are everywhere and they all wear the same uniform and use the same tools, and have the same purpose: the protection of the ruling circle here in North America. It is true that the world is one community, but we are not satisfied with the concentration of its power. We want the power for the people.

I said earlier (but I strayed away) that the theory of the "negation of the negation" is valid. Some scholars have been wondering why in Asia, Africa, and Latin America the resistance always seeks the goal of a collective society. They seem not to institute the economy of the capitalist. They seem to jump all the way from feudalism to a collective society, and some people can't understand why. Why won't they follow historical Marxism, or historical materialism? Why won't they go from feudalism to the development of a capitalistic base and finally to socialism? They don't do it because they can't do it. They don't do it for the same reason that the Black community in Harlem cannot develop capitalism, that the Black community in Oakland or San Francisco cannot develop capitalism, because the imperialists have already preempted the field. They have already centralized the wealth. Therefore, in order to deal with them all we can do is liberate our community and then move on them as a collective force.

We've had long arguments with people about our convictions. Before we became conscious we used to call ourselves a dispersed collection of colonies here in North America. And people argued with me all day and all night, asking "How can you possibly be a colony? In order to be a colony you have to have a nation, and you're not a nation, you're a community. You're a dispersed collection of communities." Because the Black Panther Party is not embarrassed to change or admit error, tonight I would like to accept the criticism and say that those critics were absolutely right. We are a collection of communities just as the Korean people, the Vietnamese people and the Chinese people are a collection of communities—a dispersed collection of communities because we have no superstructure of our own. The superstructure we have is the superstructure of Wall Street, which all of our labor produced. This is a distorted form of collectivity. Everything's been collected but it's used exclusively in the interest of the ruling circle. This is why the Black Panther Party denounces Black capitalism and says that all we can do is liberate our community, not only in Vietnam but here, not only in Cambodia and the People's Republics of China and Korea but the communities of the world. We must unite as one community and then transform the world into a place where people will be happy, wars will end, the state itself will no longer exist, and we will have communism. But we cannot do this right away. When transformation takes place, when structural change takes place, the result is usually cultural lag. After the people possess the means of production we will probably not move directly into communism but linger with Revolutionary Intercommunalism until such time as we can wash away bourgeois thought, until such time as we can wash away racism and reactionary thinking, until such time as people are not attached to their nation as a peasant is attached to the soil, until such time as that people can gain their sanity and develop a culture that is "essentially human," that will serve the people instead of some god. Because we cannot avoid contact with each other we will have to develop a value system that will help us function together in harmony.

I think I've covered tonight most of what I had to say. I will allow you to talk. We will have a question and answer period. But before I do that I would like to deliver a message to you. Our Minister of Information, Eldridge Cleaver, asked me to petition you, to ask you to prepare a place for him because he would like to return home. And also I would like to thank the peoples of the world for allowing our Minister of Information to reside in their liberated communities, in their liberated territory. So, they've actually set the example for us. We know what we have to do in order to bring Eldridge Cleaver home. We have to liberate our communities.

Resolutions and Declarations:
*December 5, 1970**

This Convention of Revolutionary Peoples from oppressed communities throughout the world is convened in recognition of the fact that changing social conditions throughout the world require new analyses and approaches in order that our consciousness might be raised to the point at which we can effectively end the oppression of people by people. We gather here from our communities because we realize that we have a common enemy, a common goal, and that the geographical barriers which separated us from one another in the past are no longer obstacles to our revolutionary unity.

Not only do we recognize our common interests, we further recognize that the concepts and ideas which were previously used to define us as peoples can no longer apply, for they dim our view and impede our progress. The same phenomena which have freed us from the separation of geographical barriers are also the same phenomena which have transformed us into a revolutionary unity.

We once defined ourselves as nations because we had distinct geographical boundaries. We controlled the economy, the political structure and the institutions in our territories. In this sense the United States was also a nation at one time.

We see, however, that the growth of bureaucratic capitalism in the United States transformed the nation. When

* An address to the Revolutionary People's Constitutional Convention held in Washington, D.C., November 28, 29, 1970.

capitalism in the nation reached a high level of development, it went beyond the national boundaries to exploit the wealth and labor of other territories. We further notice that this exploitation of the wealth of other nations included the control of their political structure and their cultural institutions. This control was maintained through the use of high levels of technology developed by bureaucratic capitalism. Technology made it possible for the strong arm of the capitalist to reach into every corner of the world and use its police force, commonly called the military, to carry out its desires. Technology also made it possible for the capitalist to control the air waves and communications media of other territories, and thereby manipulate their cultural institutions.

We recognize then that the greed of bureaucratic capitalism in America, the effectiveness of the police force of the ruling circle, and the swiftness with which their "message" can be sent to these territories has transformed the previous situation. We recognize this when we admit that the United States is no longer a nation but an empire. However, an empire, by definition, controls other countries, and in so doing transforms them. If a nation cannot protect its boundaries and prevent the entry of an aggressor, if a nation cannot control its political structure and its cultural institutions, then it is no longer a nation, it is something else. Thus our presence here is a recognition that the United States has transformed other nations into something else.

Because of this new understanding we must ally ourselves with the oppressed communities of the world. We cannot make our stand as nationalists, we cannot even make our stand as internationalists. We must place our future hopes upon the philosophy of intercommunalism, a philosophy which holds that the rise of imperialism in America transformed all other nations into oppressed communities. In revolutionary love we must make common cause with these oppressed communities.

We are aware that many of us are the descendants of those who were dispossessed of their lands to permit capitalism to flourish. We are aware that many of us are the descendants of those who were captured and enslaved so that their labor could build the wealth of this nation. But we are also aware that the capitalists used the philosophy of racism to support their wicked oppression. Through the philosophy of racism, people in this country have been taught that some citizens are better than others because of differences in physical and social characteristics, and therefore have a right to exploit the others.

This Convention of Revolutionary Peoples is gathered here to organize our forces to move against the evils of capitalism, imperialism and racism, all of which have been used to oppress people. We will move against the evil and corrupt gentry by any means necessary and sufficient to take away the power which they have wielded too selfishly for too long.

We who are gathered here by our presence do resolve to liberate our communities from the boot and whip of the oppressor so that people of good will may live their lives free from want, free from fear, and free from need. We recognize that the Chinese people, under the leadership of Mao Tse-tung; the Korean people, under the leadership of Kim I Sung; and the Algerian people under the leadership of Ben Bella rose up against the oppressor and liberated the people's territory from his hands. Consequently, oppressed individuals such as Brother Eldridge Cleaver have access to a liberated community where they can live in peace and harmony. These courageous revolutionaries have set an example for us to liberate our communities also and give freedom to those who have sought so long to bask in its glow.

There can be no real freedom until the imperialist—world-enemy-number-one—has been stripped of his power and put in his rightful place as one of the people rather than the ruler of the people. Then and only then will unity and harmony truly prevail. So we resolve to liberate our communities in order that we might serve the true interests of the community.

We who are gathered here by our presence do indicate that we believe that every community has the right to define, determine and control institutions so that they reflect the integrity of the community.

Therefore we declare that all communities of the world have the freedom to determine their own destinies. We declare that all communities, by their very existence, have the power to specify what institutions will be set up within them and what cultural values will be propagated through them. We declare that all communities have the right to determine what laws will govern their territories and what officials will be placed in leadership.

We who are gathered here do declare by our presence that the physical and social characteristics of the people of our communities shall never be used as a basis for exclusion from any aspect of life in our communities.

We declare that our goal is to destroy all elements of the oppression. We pledge ourselves to end imperialism and distribute the wealth of the world to all the people of the world. We foresee a system of true communism where all people produce according to their abilities and all receive according to their needs.

Recognizing the possibility of a cultural lag between the destruction of the oppression and the erection of a new world based on that which makes us human, we call for all people in the communities throughout the world to participate and be represented in decision making in direct proportion to their presence in the population under consideration. Whether on an intercommunal level, a regional level, or on a local level, we hold that all people have the right to proportional representation within the framework of revolutionary intercommunalism and communism.

We are here gathered for the solemn purpose of formulating a new *constitution for a new world*. We must become even more conscious of who we are and why we are in these circumstances. Then we must change these circumstances and construct a new world which makes use of all the technology and knowledge we have accumulated. When we have developed a system that functions in the true interests of the people and established it in full, then the word "work" will be re-defined as meaningful play. We will have eliminated the cause of all our problems and can live according to a Constitution of Revolutionary People.

On the Defection of Eldridge Cleaver from the Black Panther Party and the Defection of the Black Panther Party from the Black Community: April 17, 1971

The Black Panther Party bases its ideology and philosophy on a concrete analysis of concrete conditions, using dialectical materialism as our analytical method. As dialectical materialists we recognize that contradictions can lead to development. The internal struggle of opposites based upon their unity causes matter to have motion as a part of the process of development. We recognize that nothing in nature stands outside of dialectics, even the Black Panther Party. But we welcome these contradictions because they clarify and advance our struggle. We had a contradiction with our former Minister of Information, Eldridge Cleaver, but we understand this as necessary to our growth. Out of this contradiction has come new growth and a return to the original vision of the Party.

Early in the development of the Black Panther Party I wrote an essay titled "The Correct Handling of a Revolution." This was in response to another contradiction: the criticisms raised against the Party by the Revolutionary Action Movement (RAM). At that time RAM criticized us for our above-ground action: openly displaying weapons and talking about the necessity for the community to arm itself for its own self-defense. RAM said that they were underground and saw this as the correct way to handle a revolution. I responded to them by pointing out that you must establish your organization aboveground so that the people can relate to it in a way that will be positive and progressive for them. When you go underground without doing this you bury yourself so deeply that the people can neither relate to nor contact you. Then the terrorism of the underground organization will be just that—striking fear into the hearts of the very people whose interest the organization claims to be defending—because the people cannot relate to them and there is nobody there to interpret their actions. You have to set up a program of practical action and be a model for the community to follow and appreciate.

The original vision of the Party was to develop a lifeline to the people by serving their needs and defending them against their oppressors, who come to the community in many forms, from armed police to capitalist exploiters. We knew that this strategy would raise the consciousness of the people and also give us their support. Then, if we were driven underground by the oppressors the people would support us and defend us. They would know that in spite of the oppressors' interpretations our only desire was to serve their true interests, and they would defend us. In this manner we might be forced underground but there would be a lifeline to the community which would always sustain us because the people would identify with us and not with our common enemy.

For a time the Black Panther Party lost its vision and defected from the community. With the defection of Eldridge Cleaver, however, we can move again to a full-scale development of our original vision, and come out of the twilight zone which the Party has been in during the recent past.

The only reason that the Party is still in existence at this time, the only reason that we have been able to survive the repression of the Party and the murder of some of our most advanced comrades is because of the Ten-Point Program—our survival program. Our programs would be meaningless and insignificant if they were not community programs. This is why it is my opinion that as long as the Black community and oppressed people are found in North America, the Black Panther Party will last. The Party will survive as a structured vehicle because it serves the true interests of oppressed people and administers to their needs. This was the original vision of the Party. The original vision was not structured by rhetoric nor by ideology but by the practical needs of the people. And its dreamers were armed with an ideology which provided a systematic method of analysis of how best to meet those needs.

When Bobby Seale and I came together to launch the Black Panther Party, we had observed many groups. Most of them were so dedicated to rhetoric and artistic rituals that they had withdrawn from living in the twentieth century. Sometimes their analyses were beautiful but they had no practical programs which would translate these understandings to the people. When they did try to develop practical programs, they often failed because they lacked a systematic ideology which would help them make concrete analyses of concrete conditions and gain a full understanding of the community and its needs. When I was in Donald Warden's Afro-American Association, I watched him try to make a reality of community-control through Black capitalism. But Warden did not have a systematic ideology, and his attempts to initiate his program continually frustrated him and the community. They did not know why capitalism would not work for them since it had worked for other ethnic groups.

When we formed the Party, we did so because we wanted to put theory and practice together in a systematic manner. We did this through our basic Ten-Point Program. In actuality it was a Twenty-Point Program, with the practice expressed in "What We Want" and the theory expressed in "What We Believe." This program was designed to serve as a basis for a structured political vehicle.

The actions we engaged in at that time were strictly strategic actions for political purposes. They were designed to mobilize the community. Any action which does not mobilize the community toward the goal is not a revolutionary action. The action might be a marvelous statement of courage, but if it does not mobilize the people toward the goal of a higher manifestation of freedom it is not making a political statement and could even be counterrevolutionary.

We realized at a very early point in our development that *revolution is a process*. It is not a particular action, nor is it a conclusion. It is a process. This is why when feudalistic slavery wiped out chattel slavery, feudalism was revolutionary. This is why when capitalism wiped out feudalism, capitalism was revolutionary. The concrete analysis of concrete conditions will reveal the true nature of the situation and increase our understanding. This process moves in a dialectical manner and we understand the struggle of the opposites based upon their unity.

Many times people say that our Ten-Point Program is reformist, but they ignore the fact that revolution is a process. We left the program open-ended so that it could develop and people could identify with it. We did not offer it to them as a conclusion, we offered it as a vehicle to move them to a higher level. In their quest for freedom and in their attempts to prevent the oppressor from stripping them of all the things they need to exist, the people see things as moving from A to B to C; they do not see things as moving from A to Z. In other words, they have to see first some basic accomplishments in order to realize that major successes are possible. Much of the time the revolutionary will have to guide them into this understanding, but he can never take them from A to Z in one jump because it is too far ahead. Therefore, when the revolutionary begins to indulge in Z, or final conclusions, the people do not relate to him. Therefore he is no longer a revolutionary if revolution is a process. This makes any action or function which does not promote the process non-revolutionary.

When the Party went to Sacramento, when the Party faced down the policemen in front of the office of *Ramparts* Magazine, and when the Party patrolled the police with arms, we were acting at a time (1966) when the people had given up the philosophy of non-violent direct action and were beginning to deal with sterner stuff. We wanted them to see the virtues of disciplined and organized armed self-defense rather than spontaneous and disorganized outbreaks and riots. There were police-alert patrols all over the country, but we were the first *armed* police patrol. We called ourselves the Black Panther Party for Self-Defense. In all of this we had political and revolutionary objectives in mind, but we knew that we could not succeed without the support of the people.

Our strategy was based on a consistent ideology, which helped us to understand the conditions around us. We knew that the law was not prepared for what we were doing and policemen were so shocked that they didn't know what to do. We saw that the people felt a new pride and strength because of the example we set for them; and they began to look toward the vehicle we were building for answers.

Later we dropped the term "Self-Defense" from our name and just became the Black Panther Party. We discouraged actions like Sacramento and police observations because we recognized that these were not the things to do in every situation or on every occasion. We never called these revolutionary actions. The only time an action is revolutionary is when the people relate to it in a revolutionary way. If they will not use the example you set, then no matter how many guns you have your action is not revolutionary.

The gun itself is not necessarily revolutionary because the fascists carry guns, in fact they have more guns. A lot of so-called revolutionaries simply do not understand the statement by Chairman Mao that "Political power grows out of the barrel of a gun." They thought Chairman Mao said political power *is* the gun, but the emphasis is on "grows." The culmination of political power is the ownership and control of the land and the institutions thereon so that we can then get rid of the gun. That is why Chairman Mao makes the statement that "We are advocates of the abolition of war, we do not want war; but war can only be abolished through war, and in order to get rid of the gun, it is necessary to take up the gun." He is always speaking of getting rid of it. If he did not look at it in those terms, then he surely would not be revolutionary. In other words, the gun by all revolutionary principles is a tool to be used in our strategy; it is not an end in itself. This was a part of the original vision of the Black Panther Party.

I had asked Eldridge Cleaver to join the Party a number of times. But he did not join until after the confrontation with the police in front of the office of *Ramparts* Magazine, where the police were afraid to go for their guns. Without my knowledge, he took this as *the* Revolution and *the* Party. But in our basic program it was not until Point 7 that we mentioned the gun, and this was intentional. We were trying to build a political vehicle through which the people could express their revolutionary desires. We recognized that no party or organization can make the revolution, only the people can. All we could do was act as a guide to the people because revolution is a process that moves in a dialectical manner. At one point one thing might be proper, but the same action could be improper at another point. *We always emphasized a concrete analysis of conditions,* and then an appropriate response to these conditions as a way of mobilizing the people and leading them to higher levels of consciousness.

People constantly thought that we were security guards or community police. This is why we dropped the term "Self-Defense" from our name and directed the attention of the people to the fact that the only way *they* would get salvation was through *their* control of the institutions which serve the community. This would require that they organize a political vehicle which would keep their support and endorsement through its survival programs of service. They would look to it for answers and guidance. It would not be an organization which runs candidates for political office, but it would serve as a watchman over the administrators whom the people have placed in office.

Because the Black Panther Party grows out of the conditions and needs of oppressed people *we are interested in everything the people are interested in,* even though we may not see these particular concerns as the final answers to our problems. We will never run for political office, but we will endorse and support those candidates who are acting in the true interest of the people. We may even provide campaign workers for them and do voter-registration and basic precinct work. This would not be out of a commitment to electoral politics; however, it would be our way of bringing the will of the people to bear on situations in which they are interested. We will also hold such candidates responsible to the community no matter how far removed their offices may be from the community. So we lead the people by following their interests, with a view toward raising their consciousness to see beyond limited goals.

When Eldridge joined the Party it was after the police confrontation, which left him fixated with the "either-or" attitude. This was that either the community picked up the gun with the Party or else they were cowards and there was no place for them. He did not realize that if the people did not relate to the Party then there was no way that the Black Panther Party could make any revolution, for the record shows that the people are the makers of the revolution and of world history.

Sometimes there are those who express personal problems in political terms, and if they are eloquent then these personal problems can sound very political. We charge Eldridge Cleaver with this. Much of it is probably beyond his control because it is so personal. But we did not know that when he joined the Party; he was doing so only because of that act in front of *Ramparts*. We weren't trying to prove anything to ourselves. All we were trying to do, at that particular point, was to defend Betty Shabazz. But we were praised by the people.

Under the influence of Eldridge Cleaver the Party gave the community no alternative for dealing with us except by picking up the gun. This move was reactionary simply because the community was not prepared to do that at that point. Instead of being a cultural cult group we became, by that act, a revolutionary cult group. But this is a basic contradiction because revolution is a process and if the acts you commit do not fall within the scope of the process then they are non-revolutionary.

What the revolutionary movement and the Black community need is a very strong structure. This structure can only exist with the support of the people and it can only get its support through serving them. This is why we have the service to the people program—the most important thing in the Party. We will serve their needs so that they can survive through this oppression. Then when they are ready to pick up the gun, serious business will happen. Eldridge Cleaver influenced us to isolate ourselves from the Black community so that it was war between the oppressor and the Black Panther Party, not war between the oppressor and the oppressed community.

The Black Panther Party defected from the community long before Eldridge defected from the Party. Our hook-up with White radicals did not give us access to the White community because they do not guide the White community. The Black community does not relate to them so we were left in a twilight zone where we could not enter the Black community with any real political education programs; yet we were not doing anything to mobilize Whites. We had no influence in raising the consciousness of the Black community and that is the point where we defected.

We went through a free speech movement in the Party, which was unnecessary, and only further isolated us from the Black community. We had all sorts of profanity in our paper and every other word which dropped from our lips was profane. This did not happen before I was jailed because I would not stand for it, but Eldridge's influence brought it about. I do not blame him altogether; I blame the Party because the Party accepted it.

Eldridge was never fully in the leadership of the Party. Even after Bobby was snatched away from us I did not place Eldridge in a position of leadership because he was not interested in that. I made David Hilliard administrator of programs. I knew that Eldridge would not do anything to lift the consciousness of the comrades in the Party, but I knew that he could make a contribution and I pressed him to do so. I pressed him to write and edit the paper, but he wouldn't. The paper did not even come out every week until after Eldridge went to jail. But Eldridge Cleaver did make great contributions to the Black Panther Party with his writing and speaking. We want to keep this in mind because there is a positive and negative side to everything.

The correct handling of a revolution is not to offer the people an "either-or" ultimatum. Instead we must gain the support of the people through serving their needs. Then when the police or any other agency of repression tries to destroy the program, the people will move to a higher level of consciousness and action. Then the organized structure can guide the people to the point where they are prepared to deal in many ways. This was the strategy we used in 1966 when the people related to us in a positive way.

So the Black Panther Party has reached a contradiction with Eldridge Cleaver, and he has defected from the Party because we would not order everyone into the streets tomorrow to make a revolution. We recognize that this is impossible because our dialectical ideology and our analysis of concrete conditions indicate that declaring a spontaneous revolution is a fantasy. The people are not at that point now. This contradiction and conflict may seem unfortunate to some, but it is a part of the dialectical process. The resolution of this contradiction has freed us from incorrect analyses and emphases.

We are now free to move toward the building of a *community structure* which will become a true voice of the people, promoting their interests in many ways. We can continue to push our basic survival programs, we can continue to serve the people as advocates of their true interests, we can truly become a political revolutionary vehicle which will lead the people to a higher level of consciousness so that they will know what they must really do in their quest for freedom. Then they will have the courage to adopt any means necessary to seize the time and obtain that freedom.

The original vision of the Black Panther Party was to serve the needs of the oppressed people in our communities and defend them against their oppressors. When the Party was initiated we knew that these goals would raise the consciousness of the people and motivate them to move more firmly for their total liberation. We also recognized that we live in a country which has become one of the most repressive governments in the world; repressive in communities all over the world. We did not expect such a repressive government to stand idly by while the Black Panther Party went forward to the goal of serving the people. We expected repression.

We knew, as a revolutionary vanguard, repression would be the reaction of our oppressors, but we recognized that the task of the revolutionist is difficult and his life is short. We were prepared then, as we are now, to give our all in the interest of oppressed people. We expected the repression to come from outside forces which have long held our communities in subjection. However, the ideology of dialectical materialism helped us to understand that the contradictions surrounding the Party would create a force that would move us toward our goals. We also expected contradictions within the Party, for the oppressors use infiltrators and provocateurs to help them reach their evil ends. Even when the contradictions come from formerly loyal members of the Party, we see them as part of the process of development rather than in the negative terms the oppressors' media use to interpret them. Above all, we knew that through it all the Party would survive.

The Party would survive because it had the love and support of the people who saw their true interests expressed in the actions of the Party. The Party would also survive because it would be a political vehicle which continued to voice the interests of the people and serve as their advocates.

The importance of a structured political vehicle has always been apparent to us. When we went to Sacramento, we went for the purpose of educating the people and building of a permanent political vehicle to serve their true interests. In our most recent communication with both the North and South Vietnamese Revolutionary governments, they pointed out that they understood what we were doing and saw it as the correct strategy. They said that a "structured organization is related to politics as a shadow to a man." We recognize that the political machine in America has consistently required Black people to support it through paying taxes and fighting in wars, but that same machine consistently refuses to serve the interests of the Black community. One of the problems is that the community does not have a structured organization or vehicle which serves its needs and represents the people's interest. You can no more have effective politics without a structured organization than you can have a man without his shadow. Oppressed Black people—*the lumpenproletariat*—did not have a structured organization to represent their true interests until the Black Panther Party arose from within the community, motivated by the needs and conditions of the people.

Across the country there have been coalitions of Black people and Black caucuses, but these have not served the people as political vehicles. They have merely served as bourgeois structures to get Black candidates into political office. Once elected, the machinery used to thrust these people into office simply passed out of existence or became ineffective insofar as serving the true interests of the Black oppressed people.

A truly revolutionary vehicle which will survive the repression it encounters daily is made up of a number of characteristics. First of all, there is a small but dedicated *cadre of workers who are willing to devote their full time to the goals of the organization.* Secondly, there is a distinct organized structure through which the cadre can function. It is this combination of structure and dedicated cadre which can maintain the machinery for meeting the people's needs. In this way a printing press can be maintained to review the events of the day and interpret them in a manner which serves the people. Information can be circulated about daily phenomena to inform the people of their true meaning. Programs of service can be carried out to deliver to the people the basic needs that are not met elsewhere because the lumpenproletariat are the victims of oppression and exploitation. A cadre and a structure, however, are not what make the political vehicle a revolutionary one. It is the revolutionary concepts which define and interpret phenomena, and establish the goals toward which the political vehicle will work. A revolutionary vehicle is in fact a revolutionary concept set into motion by a dedicated cadre through a particular organized structure.

Such a vehicle can survive repression because it can move in the necessary manner at the appropriate time. It can go underground if the conditions require, and it can rise up again. But it will always be motivated by love and dedication to the interests of the oppressed communities. Therefore the people will insure its survival, for only in that survival are their needs serviced. The structured and organized vehicle will guarantee the weathering of the test of internal and external contradictions.

The responsibility of such a political vehicle is clear. It is to function as a machine which serves the true interests of the oppressed people. This means that it must be ever aware of the needs of the communities of the oppressed and develop and execute the necessary programs to meet those needs. The Black Panther Party has done this through its basic Ten-Point Program. However, we recognize that *revolution is a process and we cannot offer the people conclusions*—we must be ready to respond creatively to new conditions and new understandings. Therefore, we have developed our Free Breakfast Program, our Free Health Clinics, our Clothing and Shoe Programs, and our Buses to Prisons Program as well as others, responding to the obvious needs of Black people. The overwhelmingly favorable response to these programs in every community is evidence that they are serving the true interests of the people.

Serving the true interests of the people also means that the political vehicle must stand between the people and the oppressive forces which prey upon them in such a manner that the administrators will have to give the appropriate response. Such articulation requires us to have a political organ which will express the interests of the people and interpret phenomena for them. Again, the existence of such a political vehicle is justified only so long as it serves the true interests of the people.

Serving the true interests of the people, however, does not mean that the vehicle is simply a reflector of public opinion, for the opinions of the people have often been molded and directed against their true interests by slick politicians and exploitative educators. Their diversion tactics often lead the people down blind alleys or onto tangents which take them away from their true goals. We can easily see this when we apply the concept of American democracy to the Black community.

Democracy in America (bourgeois democracy) means nothing more than the domination of the majority over the minority. That is why Black people can cast votes all year long but if the majority is against us, we suffer. Then the politicians and educators try to deceive the community with statements such as "It's rule by the majority, but the rights of the minority are protected." If, in fact, participating in the democratic process in America were in the interest of the Black community there would be no need for a Free Breakfast Program, there would be no need for Free Health Clinics or any of the other programs we have developed to meet the people's needs. The rights of the minority are "protected" by the standards of a bourgeois government, and anything which is not in their interest is not permitted. This may be democratic for the majority, but for the minority it has the same effect as fascism. When the majority decreed that we should be slaves, we were slaves—where was the democracy in slavery for us? When the majority decreed that we should pay taxes, fight and die in wars, and be given inferior and racist education against our interests, we got all of these things. Where is democracy for us in any of that? Our children still die, our youth still suffer from malnutrition, our middle-aged people still suffer from sickle-cell anemia, and our elderly still face unbearable poverty and hardship because they reach the twilight period of their lives with nothing to sustain them through these difficult times. Where is the democracy in any of this for Black people? Democracy means only that the majority will use us when they need us and cast us aside when they do not need us. A true understanding of the working and effect of American democracy for Black people will reveal most clearly that it is just the same as fascism for us. Our true interests and needs are not being served.

The political vehicle of the people must be guided by a consistent ideology which represents nothing more than a systematic and organized set of principles for analyzing and interpreting objective phenomena. An ideology can only be accepted as valid if it delivers a true understanding of the phenomena which affect the lives of the people. The development of a wide variety of truths about the community, its internal development and the external forces surrounding it will lead then to a philosophy which will help orient us toward goals which are in the true interests of the people.

The Black Panther Party was born in a period of stress when Black people were moving away from the philosophy and strategy of non-violent action toward sterner actions. We dared to believe that we could offer the community a permanent political vehicle which would serve their needs and advocate their interests. We have met many foes; we have seen many enemies. We have been slandered, kidnapped, gagged, jailed and murdered. We know now, more than ever before, that the will of the people is greater than the technology and repression of those who are against the interests of the people. Therefore we know that we can and will continue to serve and educate the people.

On the Relevance of the Church:
*May 19, 1971**

Since 1966 the Black Panther Party has gone through many changes; it has been transformed. I would like to talk to you about that and about contradictions. I would also like to talk about the Black Panther Party's relationship with the community as a whole and with the church in particular.

Some time ago when the Party started, Bobby and I were interested in strengthening the Black community— rather its comprehensive set of institutions because if there is one thing we lack it is community. We do have one institution that has been around for some time and that is the church. After a short harmonious relationship with the church, in fact a very good relationship, we were divorced from the church, and shortly after that found ourselves out of favor with the whole Black community.

We found ourselves in somewhat of a void alienated from the whole community. We had no way of being effective as far as developing the community was concerned. The only way we could aid in that process of revolution— and revolution is a process rather than conclusion or a set of principles, or any particular action—was by raising the consciousness of the community. Any conclusion or particular action that we think *is* revolution is really reaction, for revolution is a developmental process. It has a forward thrust which goes higher and higher as man becomes freer and freer. As man becomes freer he knows more about the

* Delivered at the Center for Urban Black Studies, Graduate Theological Union, Berkeley, California.

universe, he tends to control more and he therefore gains more control over himself. That is what freedom is all about.

I want now to talk about the mistakes that were made. I hate to call them mistakes because maybe they were necessary to bring about change in the Party, the needed transformation. I am sure that we will have other kinds of contradictions in the future, some that we don't know about now. I am sure they will build up and hurl us into a new thing.

But the church also has been going through phases of development. It too has found itself somewhat isolated from the community. Today, the church is striving to get back into favor with the community. Like the church the Black Panther Party is also trying to reinstate itself with the community.

A short time ago there was an article in the Black Panther paper called "The Defection of Eldridge Cleaver from the Black Panther Party and the Defection of the Black Panther Party from the Black Community." I would like to concentrate now upon the defection of the Party. That is, the larger unit. I hate to place blame upon individuals in our Party particularly since they are always governed by a collective called the Central Committee. Even when I disagree with the Central Committee (and I did much disagreeing and arguing when I was in prison, but I was out-voted), after the vote I supported the position of the Party until the next meeting.

I think, at first, that we have to have some organized apparatus in order to bring about the necessary change. The only time we leave our political machine or our institution altogether is when we feel that we cannot bring about the necessary change through the machine, and the very posture of the organization or the institution will strip us of our individual dignity. I felt that this was true of the Party, and although it could be argued, *I personally thought that the Party should still be held together.* I knew if I left we would have to form a new Party, a new institution in order to be that spur or that guiding light in the community. Also I would have to contend with new contradictions.

We always say that contradictions are the ruling principle of the universe. I use that word time and time again because I think that it is responsible for much suffering. When things collide they hurt, but collision is also responsible for development. Without contradictions everything would be stagnant. Everything has an internal contradiction including the church.

Contradiction, or the strain of the lesser to subdue that which controls it, gives motion to matter. We see this throughout the universe in the physical as well as the biological world. We also see this in cultures. Development comes with the phenomenon we call acculturation. That is, two societies meet and when their cultures collide because they have a contradiction, both are modified. The stronger shows less change and the weaker more change. All the time the weaker is attempting to gain dominance over the stronger. But something happens, they both will never be the same again because they have reached a degree of synthesis. In other words, it is all working toward the truth of the trinity: thesis, anti-thesis, synthesis. This principle of contradiction, this striving for harmony, operates in all of our disciplines.

The Black Panther Party was formed because we wanted to oppose the evils in our community. Some of the members in the Party were not refined—we were grasping for organization. It wasn't a college campus organization; it was basically an organization of the grass roots, and any time we organize the most victimized of the victims we run into a problem. To have a Party or a church or any kind of institution, whether we like it or not, we have to have administrators. How an institution, organization, or the Party in this case, functions, as well as how effective it is depends upon how knowledgeable and advanced in thinking the administrators are. We attempt to apply the administrative skills of our grass-roots organization to the problems that are most frequently heard in the community.

History shows that most of the parties that have led people out of their difficulties have had administrators with what we sometimes call the traits of the bourgeoisie or de-classed intellectuals. They are the people who have gone through the established institutions, rejected them, and then applied their skills to the community. In applying them to the community, their skills are no longer bourgeoisie skills but people's skills, which are transformed through the contradiction of applying what is usually bourgeoisie to the oppressed. That itself is a kind of transformation.

In our Party we are not so blessed. History does not repeat itself; it goes on also transforming itself through its dialectical process. We see that the administrators of our Party are victims who have not received that bourgeois training. So I will not apologize for our mistakes, our lack of a scientific approach to use and put into practice. It was a matter of not knowing, of learning, but also of starting out with a loss—a disadvantage that history has seldom seen. That is, a group attempting to influence and change the society so much while its own administrators were as much in the dark much of the time as the people that they were trying to change. In our Party we have now what we call the Ideological Institute, where we are teaching these skills, and we also invite those people who have received a bourgeois education to come and help us. However we let them know that they will, by their contribution, make their need to exist, as they exist now, null and void. In other words, after we learn the skills their bourgeois status will evaporate once the skills have been applied.

As far as the church was concerned, the Black Panther Party and other community groups emphasized the political and criticized the spiritual. We said the church is only a

ritual, it is irrelevant, and therefore we will have nothing to
do with it. We said this in the context of the whole community being involved with the church on one level or another.
That is one way of defecting from the community, and that
is exactly what we did. Once we stepped outside of the
church with that criticism, we stepped outside of the whole
thing that the community was involved in and we said,
"You follow our example; your reality is not true and you
don't need it."

Now, without judging whether the church is operating in
a total reality, I will venture to say that if we judge whether
the church is relevant to the *total* community we would all
agree that it is not. That is why it develops new programs—
to become more relevant so the pews will be filled on
Sunday.

The church is in its developmental process, and we
believe it needs to exist. We believe this as a result of our
new direction (which is an old direction as far as I am
concerned, but we'll call it new because there has been a
reversal in the dominance in the Central Committee of our
Party for reasons that you probably know about). So we do
go to church, are involved in the church, and not in any
hypocritical way. Religion, perhaps, is a thing that man
needs at this time because scientists cannot answer all of the
questions. As far as I am concerned, when all of the questions are not answered, when the extraordinary is not
explained, when the unknown is not known, then there is
room for God because the unexplained and the unknown *is*
God. We know nothing about God, really, and that is why
as soon as the scientist develops or points out a new way of
controlling a part of the universe, that aspect of the universe is no longer God. In other words, once when the
thunder crashed it was God clapping His hands together. As
soon as we found out that thunder was not God, we said
that God has other attributes but not *that* one. In that way
we took for ourselves what was His before. But we still

haven't answered all of the questions, so He still exists. And those scientists who say they can answer all of them are dishonest.

We go into the church realizing that we cannot answer the questions at this time, that the answers will be delivered eventually, and we feel that when they are delivered they will be explained in a way that we can understand and control.

I went to church for years. My father is a minister and I spent 15 years in the church; this was my life as a child. When I was going to church I used to hear that God is within us and is, therefore, some part of us: that part of us that is mystical. And as man develops and understands more, he will approach God, and finally reach heaven and merge with the universe. I've never heard one preacher say that there is a need for the church in heaven; the church would negate itself. As man approaches his development and becomes larger and larger, the church therefore becomes smaller and smaller because it is not needed any longer. Then if we had ministers who would deal with the social realities that cause misery so that we can change them, man will become larger and larger. At that time the God within will come out, and we can merge with Him. Then we will be one with the universe.

So I think it was rather arrogant of my Party to criticize the community for trying to discover answers to spiritual questions. The only thing we will criticize in the future is when the church does not act upon the evils that cause man to get on his knees and humble himself in awe at that large force which he cannot control. But as man becomes stronger and stronger, and his understanding greater and greater, he will have "a closer walk with Thee." *Note the song says walk—not crawl.*

So along with the church we will all start again to control our lives and communities. Even with the Black church we have to create a community spirit. We say that the church is an institution, but it is not a community. The sociological definition of a community is a comprehensive *collection* of institutions that delivers our whole life, and within which we can reach most of our goals. We create it in order to carry out our desires and it serves us. In the Black community the church is an institution that we created (that we were allowed to create). The White church warred against us, but finally we won the compromise to worship as a unit, as a people, concerned with satisfying our own needs. The White church was not satisfying our needs in human terms because it felt that we were not human beings. So we formed our own. Through that negative thing a positive thing evolved. We started to organize fraternities, anti-lynching groups and so forth, but they still would not let our community exist. We came here in chains and I guess they thought we were meant to stay in chains. But we have begun to organize a political machine, to develop a community so that we can have an apparatus to fight back. You cannot fight back individually against an organized machine. We will work with the church to establish a community which will satisfy most of our needs so that we can live and operate as a group.

The Black Panther Party, with its survival programs, plans to develop the institutions in the community. We have a clothing factory we are just erecting on Third Street, where we will soon give away about three hundred to four hundred new articles of clothing each month. And we can do this by robbing Peter to pay Paul. What we will do is start to make golfing bags under contract to a company, and with the surplus we will buy material to make free clothes. Our members will do this. We will have no overhead because of our collective (we'll "exploit" our collective by making them work free). We will do this not just to satisfy ourselves, like the philanthropist, or to serve, or to save someone from going without shoes, even though this is a part of the cause of our problem, but to help the people make the revolution. We will give the process a forward thrust. If we suffer genocide we won't be around to change things. So in this way our survival program is very practical.

What we are concerned with is the larger problem. Therefore we will be honest and say that we will do like the churches—we will negate our necessity for existing. After we accomplish our goals the Black Panther Party will not need to exist because we will have already created our heaven right here on earth. What we are going to do is administer to the community the things they need in order to get their attention, in order to organize them into a political machine. The community will then look to the Party and look to those people who are serving their needs in order to give them guidance and direction, whether it is political, whether it is judicial, or whether it is economic.

Our real thing is to organize across the country. We have thirty-eight chapters and branches and I would like to inform you that the so-called split is only a myth, that it does not exist. We lost two chapters in that so-called split and I will tell you that the burden is off my shoulders. I was glad to lose them because it was a yoke for me; I was frozen. Even though I couldn't make a move I wouldn't get out of the whole thing then because certain people had such an influence over the Party. For me to have taken that stand would have been individualism. Now we're about three years behind in our five-year plan, but we will *now* move to organize the community around the *survival* programs.

We have a shoe factory that we're opening up on 14th and Jefferson. The machines and everything else were donated. We'll use it to get inmates out of prison because most of us learned how to make shoes in prison. So it will serve two purposes: we can make positions in the shoe factory available and thereby get somebody out on parole; and since the parolees must agree to give a certain amount of shoes away each week, we will have a "right to wear shoes" program. We'll point out that everyone in the society should have shoes and we should not have a situation like the one in Beaufort County, South Carolina, where 70 percent of the children suffer brain damage because of malnutrition. They have malnutrition because of the combination of not enough food and parasites in the stomach. The worms eat up half the food that the children take in. Why? Because the ground is infested with the eggs of the worms and the children don't have shoes to wear. So as soon as we send a doctor there to cure them, they get the parasites again. We think that a shoe program is a very relevant thing, first to help them stay alive, then to create conditions in which they can grow up and work out a plan to change things. If they have brain damage, they will never be revolutionists because they will have already been killed. That is genocide in itself.

We will inform this government, this social order, that it must administer to its people because it is supposed to be a representative government which serves the needs of the people. Then serve them. If it does not do this then it should be criticized. What we will not do in the future is jump too far ahead and say that the system absolutely cannot give us anything. That is not true; the system can correct itself to a certain extent. What we are interested in is its correcting itself as much as it can. After that, if it doesn't do everything that the people think necessary, then we'll think about reorganizing things.

To be very honest I think there is great doubt whether the present system can do this. But until the people feel the same way I feel then I would be rather arrogant to say dump the whole thing, just as we were arrogant to say dump the church. Let's give it a chance, let's work with it in order to squeeze as many contributions and compromises out of all the institutions as possible, and then criticize them after the fact. We'll know when that time comes, when the people tell us so.

We have a program attempting to get the people to do all they will do. It is too much to ask the people to do all they can do even though they can do everything. But that is not the point. The point is how do we get them to do all they *will* do until they eventually get to the place where they will have to be doing all they can.

We organized the Party when we saw that growing out of the Movement was what was called a cultural cult group. We defined a cultural cult group as an organization that disguised itself as a political organization, but was really more interested in the cultural rituals of Africa in the 1100's before contact with the Europeans. Instead of administering to the community and organizing it, they would rather wear bubas, get African names and demand that the community do the same, and do nothing about the survival of the community. Sometimes they say, "Well, if we get our culture back then all things will be solved." This is like saying to be regenerated and born again is to solve everything. We know that this is not true.

Then the Party became just as closed as the cultural cultist group. You know many churches that are very reactionary which you describe as a religious cult. They go through many rituals but they're divorced from reality. Even though we have many things in common with them, we say they isolate themselves from reality because they're so miserable and reality is so hard to take. We know that operating within reality does not mean that we accept it; we're operating within it so that the reality can be changed. For what we did as revolutionists was abstract, and the people are always real. But we know that reality is changing all the time, and what we want to do is harness those forces that are causing the change to direct them to a desirable goal. In other words developments will continue, but we have no guarantee that they will be developments that allow man to live. We have no guarantee that the bomb won't be dropped, but we know that there are certain ways

that we can plan for the new reality. In order to do this we
have to take some control over the present. So the people
who withdraw, like the religious cultist group, do the same
thing as the cultural cultist group.

These are words that we have coined. The Panthers are
always coining words because we have to keep defining the
new reality, the new phenomena. The old words confuse us
sometimes because things have changed so much. So we try
to stay abreast by developing or stipulating definitions. The
old lexical definitions become so outdated after the qualitative leap (the transformation) that it does not match at
all what we are talking about now.

One new word related to what we have been talking
about describes something I was guilty of. I was guilty of
this when I offered the Black troops to Vietnam. I won't talk
about whether it was morally right or wrong, but I will say
that anything said or done by a revolutionist that does not
spur or give the forward thrust to the process (of revolution) is wrong. Remember that the people are the makers of
history, the people make everything in their society. They
are the architects of the society and if you don't spur them
on, then I don't care what phrases you use or whether they
are political or religious, you cannot be classified as being
relevant to that process. If you know you're wrong and do
certain things anyway, then you're reactionary because you
are very very guilty. You deserve many stripes. Some of us
didn't know. I keep searching myself to see whether I knew
we were going wrong. I couldn't influence the Central
Committee and maybe I should have risked being charged
with an individual violation and said that they didn't know.
I think most of them didn't know, so they're not as guilty as
I am. I'm probably more guilty than anyone. But anyway,
the new word that describes what we went into for a short
length of time—a couple of years—is revolutionary
cultism.

The revolutionary cultist uses the words of social change;

he uses words about being interested in the development of society. He uses that terminology, you see; but his actions are so far divorced from the process of revolution and organizing the community that he is living in a fantasy world. So we talk to each other on the campuses, or we talk to each other in the secrecy of the night, concentrating upon weapons, thinking these things will produce change without the people themselves. Of course people do courageous things and call themselves the vanguard, but the people who do things like that are either heroes or criminals. They are not the vanguard because the vanguard means spearhead, and the spearhead has to spearhead something. If nothing is behind it, then it is divorced from the masses and is not the vanguard.

I am going to be heavily criticized now by the revolutionary cultists and probably criticized even more in the future because I view the process as going in stages. I feel that we can't jump from A to Z, we have to go through all of the development. So even though I see a thing is not the answer, I don't think it's dishonest to involve myself in it for the simple reason that the people tend to take not one step higher; they take a half step higher. Then they hang on to what they view as the reality because they can't see that reality is constantly changing. When they finally see the changes (qualitatively) they don't know why or how it happened. Part of the reason reality changes around them is because they are there; they participate whether they like it or not.

What we will do now is involve ourselves in any thing or any stage of development in the community, support that development, and try to introduce some insight into it. Then we will work very hard with the people in the community and with this institution so that it can negate itself. We will be honest about this and we hope they are honest too and realize that everything is negated eventually; this is how we go on to higher levels.

I was warned when I got up here that it would be appropriate to have a question and answer period, so I guess we should start now because I'm subject to go on and on.

QUESTION: I would like to know in your re-evaluation of your former stance in relationship to the community, in what ways do you expect to merge or bring together the community of the Catholic Church into the Black Panther Party?

NEWTON: First, we can't change the realities, direct them, or harness their forces until we know them. We have to gather information. We can gather information about the church by experiencing the church. As a matter of fact this is how we gain facts: through empirical evidence, observation, and experience. In order to do this we have to go to the church. You see, the only laboratory in society we have is the community itself, and we view ourselves not only as scientists but also as activists.

Now we say we try to merge theory with practice, so we're going to churches now. I went to church last week for the first time in ten years, I guess. We took our children with us. We have a youth institute, the Samuel Napier Youth Institute. We have about thirty children now and we took them to church and involved ourselves. We plan to involve ourselves in many community activities, going through the behavior the church goes through in order to contribute to the community. We also hope to influence the church, as I'm sure the church will influence us. Remember that we said that even when whole societies and cultures meet they are both modified by each other. And I am saying that the very fact that we're there is the new ingredient in the church, and we know that we will be affected and hope that they will be affected. But I warn you that we hope to have more effect than they.

Just briefly I mentioned our Youth Institute. We have children from three to fourteen years old; most of them have already been kicked out of schools and we have a shortage of facilities because the hard core Black community is just an aggregate now. People who happen to be Black.

We are teaching them first what I mentioned earlier, bourgeois skills. It is necessary for us to learn these skills in order to understand the phenomena around us, the society. On the other hand, we don't like the way the skills have been used, so we're going to use them a different way. Thirdly, our children are not going to withdraw. I don't like parochial schools; I don't like separate schools, but I think that sometimes you have to use that strategy. For example, the Black Panther Party is a Black organization. We know that we live in a world of many cultures and ethnic groups and we all interconnect in one way or another. We say that we are the contradiction to the reactionary Western values, but we cannot separate because we're here. Technology is too far advanced for us to isolate ourselves in any geographical location—the jet can get there too fast and so can the early-bird TV set—so what we have to do is share the control of these devices.

So far as our children are concerned, the only reason they are at this separate school is because the public schools were not giving them the correct education. They can hardly learn to read and write. I don't want them to end up as I did: I only learned how to read after I was seventeen and that must not happen to them. I've only been reading for about 10 years or so and that is not very good—I still don't read very well. Our plan is not to have our children graduate from our school and live in a fantasy. Our effort is to keep them in there just as long as it will take for them to organize the school and make it relevant. In other words we are going to send them back into the wilderness, but we're going to send them with their purse and their scribes with them this time.

QUESTION: When David Hilliard spoke to the National

Committee of Black Churchmen that met in Berkeley, he called the preachers who were gathered there a bunch of bootlicking pimps and motherfuckers, a comment that never should have been made public anyway. And he threatened that if the preachers did not come around that the Panthers would "off" some of the preachers. If you're not able to influence the Black church as much as you think, will the Panther Party return to this particular stance?

NEWTON: The Black Panther Party will not take the separate individual stand. We'll only take the stand of the community because we're interested in what the community will do to liberate themselves. We will not be arrogant and we would not have the most rudimentary knowledge if we did not know that we alone cannot bring about change. It was very wrong and almost criminal for some people in the Party to make the mistake to think that the Black Panther Party could overthrow even the police force. It ended up with the war between the police and the Panthers, and if there is a war it needs to be between the community and the reactionary establishment, or else we are isolating ourselves.

As for what David Hilliard said, what he did was alienate you. That kind of alienation put us in a void where blood was spilled from one end of this country to the other, our blood, while the community watched. Our help watched on, you see? But it was more our fault than theirs because we were out there saying that we were going to lead them into a change. But we cannot lead them into a change if they will not go. As a matter of fact, we cannot exist individually if we don't band together to resist the genocide against all of us. So just as I criticize David Hilliard, I criticize myself, because I knew that stuff was going on and I argued against it, but I didn't leave the Party. Finally the change came about.

And so what I am saying is that I understand, and the

reason that I didn't leave was that it wasn't an outrage to my humanity even though I cringed every time. Because I understood that he did it not out of hatred, but love. He did it because he was outraged by the church's inactivity, as you are outraged (not you personally, but you in the plural) at this situation, and he was outraged, of course, because of your isolation. So we are all in the same boat; and when we end up in the same boat that means we are unified.

II

The People

*The people will rise like
a mighty storm.*

BLACK AMERICA

Fear and Doubt:
May 15, 1967

The lower socio-economic Black male is a man of confusion. He faces a hostile environment and is not sure that it is not his own sins that have attracted the hostilities of society. All his life he has been taught (explicitly and implicitly) that he is an inferior approximation of humanity. As a man, he finds himself void of those things that bring respect and a feeling of worthiness. He looks around for something to blame for his situation, but because he is not sophisticated regarding the socio-economic milieu and because of negativistic parental and institutional teachings, he ultimately blames himself.

When he was a child his parents told him that they were not affluent because "we didn't have the opportunity to become educated," or "we did not take advantage of the educational opportunities that were offered to us." They tell their children that things will be different for them if they are educated and skilled but there is absolutely nothing other than this occasional warning (and often not even this) to stimulate education. Black people are great worshipers of education, even the lower socio-economic Black person, but at the same time they are afraid of exposing themselves to it. They are afraid because they are vulnerable to having their fears verified; perhaps they will find that they can't compete with White students. The Black person tells himself that he could have done much more if he had really wanted to. The fact is, of course, that the assumed educational opportunities were never available to the lower socio-economic Black person due to the unique position assigned him in life.

It is a two-headed monster that haunts this man. First, his attitude is that he lacks the innate ability to cope with the socio-economic problems confronting him, and second, he tells himself that he has the ability, but he simply has not felt strongly enough to try to acquire the skills needed to manipulate his environment. In a desperate effort to assume self-respect he rationalizes that he is lethargic; in this way, he denies a possible lack of innate ability. If he openly attempts to discover his abilities he and others may see him for what he is—or is not—and this is the real fear. He then withdraws into the world of the invisible, but not without a struggle. He may attempt to make himself visible by processing his hair, acquiring a "boss mop," or driving a long car even though he cannot afford it. He may father several "illegitimate" children by several different women in order to display his masculinity. But in the end, he realizes that his efforts have no real effect.

Society responds to him as a thing, a beast, a nonentity, something to be ignored or stepped on. He is asked to respect laws that do not respect him. He is asked to digest a code of ethics that acts upon him, but not for him. He is confused and in a constant state of rage, of shame, of doubt. This psychological state permeates all his interpersonal relationships. It determines his view of the social system. His psychological development has been prematurely arrested. This doubt begins at a very early age and continues throughout his life. The parents pass it on to the child and the social system reinforces the fear, the shame, and the doubt. In the third or fourth grade he may find that he shares the classroom with White students, but when the class is engaged in reading exercises, all the Black students find themselves in a group at a table reserved for slow readers. This may be quite an innocent effort on the part of the school system. The teacher may not realize that the Black students feared (in fact, feel certain) that Black means dumb, and White means smart. The children do not realize that the head start White children get at home is what accounts for the situation. It is generally accepted that the child is the father of the man; this holds true for the lower socio-economic Black people.

With whom, with what can he, a man, identify? As a child he had no permanent male figure with whom to identify; as a man, he sees nothing in society with which he can identify as an extension of himself. His life is built on mistrust, shame, doubt, guilt, inferiority, role confusion, isolation and despair. He feels that he is something less than a man, and it is evident in his conversation: "The White man is 'THE MAN,' he got everything, and he knows everything, and a nigger ain't nothing." In a society where a man is valued according to occupation and material possessions, he is without possessions. He is unskilled and more often than not, either marginally employed or unemployed. Often his wife (who is able to secure a job as a maid, cleaning for White people) is the breadwinner. He is, therefore, viewed as quite worthless by his wife and children. He is ineffectual both in and out of the home. He cannot provide for, or protect his family. He is invisible, a nonentity. Society will not acknowledge him as a man. He is a consumer and not a producer. He is dependent upon the White man ("THE MAN") to feed his family, to give him a job, educate his children, serve as the model that he tries to emulate. He is dependent and he hates "THE MAN" and he hates himself. Who is he? Is he a very old adolescent or is he the slave he used to be?

"What did he do to be so Black and blue?"

From "In Defense of Self-Defense" I: June 20, 1967

Men were not created in order to obey laws. Laws are created to obey men. They are established by men and should serve men. The laws and rules which officials inflict upon poor people prevent them from functioning harmoniously in society. There is no disagreement about this function of law in any circle—the disagreement arises from the question of which men laws are to serve. Such lawmakers ignore the fact that it is the duty of the poor and unrepresented to construct rules and laws that serve their interests better. Rewriting unjust laws is a basic human right and fundamental obligation.

Before 1776 America was a British colony. The British Government had certain laws and rules that the colonized Americans rejected as not being in their best interests. In spite of the British conviction that Americans had no right to establish their own laws to promote the general welfare of the people living here in America, the colonized immigrant felt he had no choice but to raise the gun to defend his welfare. Simultaneously he made certain laws to ensure his protection from external and internal aggressions, from other governments, and his own agencies. One such form of protection was the Declaration of Independence, which states: ". . . whenever any government becomes destructive to these ends, it is the right of the people to alter or to abolish it, and to institute a new government, laying its foundations on such principles and organizing its powers in such forms as to them shall seem most likely to effect their safety and happiness."

Now these same colonized White people, these bondsmen, paupers, and thieves deny the colonized Black man not only the right to abolish this oppressive system, but to even *speak* of abolishing it. Having carried this madness and cruelty to the four corners of the earth, there is now universal rebellion against their continued rule and power. But as long as the wheels of the imperialistic war machine are turning, there is no country that can defeat this monster of the West. It is our belief that the Black people in America are the only people who can free the world, loosen the yoke of colonialism, and destroy the war machine. Black people who are within the machine can cause it to malfunction. They can, because of their intimacy with the mechanism, destroy the engine that is enslaving the world. America will not be able to fight every Black country in the world and fight a civil war at the same time. It is militarily impossible to do both of these things at once.

The slavery of Blacks in this country provides the oil for the machinery of war that America uses to enslave the peoples of the world. Without this oil the machinery cannot function. We are the driving shaft; we are in such a strategic position in this machinery that, once we become dislocated, the functioning of the remainder of the machinery breaks down.

Penned up in the ghettos of America, surrounded by his factories and all the physical components of his economic system, we have been made into "the wretched of the earth," relegated to the position of spectators while the White racists run their international con game on the suffering peoples. We have been brainwashed to believe that we are powerless and that there is nothing we can do for ourselves to bring about a speedy liberation for our people. We have been taught that we must please our oppressors, that we are only ten percent of the population, and therefore must confine our tactics to categories calculated not to disturb the sleep of our tormentors.

The power structure inflicts pain and brutality upon the

peoples and then provides controlled outlets for the pain in ways least likely to upset them, or interfere with the process of exploitation. The people must repudiate the established channels as tricks and deceitful snares of the exploiting oppressors. The people must oppose everything the oppressor supports, and support everything that he opposes. If Black people go about their struggle for liberation in the way that the oppressor dictates and sponsors, then we will have degenerated to the level of groveling flunkies for the oppressor himself. When the oppressor makes a vicious attack against freedom-fighters because of the way that such freedom-fighters choose to go about their liberation, then we know we are moving in the direction of our liberation. The racist dog oppressors have no rights which oppressed Black people are bound to respect. As long as the racist dogs pollute the earth with the evil of their actions, they do not deserve any respect at all, and the "rules" of their game, written in the people's blood, are beneath contempt.

The oppressor must be harassed until his doom. He must have no peace by day or by night. The slaves have always outnumbered the slavemasters. The power of the oppressor rests upon the submission of the people. When Black people really unite and rise up in all their splendid millions, they will have the strength to smash injustice. We do not understand the power in our numbers. We are millions and millions of Black people scattered across the continent and throughout the Western Hemisphere. There are more Black people in America than the total population of many countries now enjoying full membership in the United Nations. They have power and their power is based primarily on the fact that they are organized and united with each other. They are recognized by the powers of the world.

We, with all our numbers, are recognized by no one. In fact, we do not even recognize our own selves. We are unaware of the potential power latent in our numbers. In 1967, in the midst of a hostile racist nation whose hidden racism is rising to the surface at a phenomenal speed, we are still so blind to our critical fight for our very survival that we are continuing to function in petty, futile ways. Divided, confused, fighting among ourselves, we are still in the elementary stage of throwing rocks, sticks, empty wine bottles and beer cans at racist police who lie in wait for a chance to murder unarmed Black people. The racist police have worked out a system for suppressing these spontaneous rebellions that flare up from the anger, frustration, and desperation of the masses of Black people. We can no longer afford the dubious luxury of the terrible casualties wantonly inflicted upon us by the police during these rebellions.

Black people must now move, from the grass roots up through the perfumed circles of the Black bourgeoisie, to seize by any means necessary a proportionate share of the power vested and collected in the structure of America. We must organize and unite to combat by long resistance the brutal force used against us daily. The power structure depends upon the use of force within retaliation. This is why they have made it a felony to teach guerrilla warfare. This is why they want the people unarmed.

The racist dog oppressors fear the armed people; they fear most of all Black people armed with weapons and the ideology of the Black Panther Party for Self-Defense. An unarmed people are slaves or are subject to slavery at any given moment. If a government is not afraid of the people it will arm the people against foreign aggression. Black people are held captive in the midst of their oppressors. There is a world of difference between thirty million unarmed submissive Black people and thirty million Black people armed with freedom, guns, and the strategic methods of liberation.

When a mechanic wants to fix a broken-down car engine, he must have the necessary tools to do the job. When the people move for liberation they must have the basic tool of liberation: the gun. Only with the power of the gun can the Black masses halt the terror and brutality directed against them by the armed racist power structure; and in one sense only by the power of the gun can the whole world be transformed into the earthly paradise dreamed of by the people from time immemorial. One successful practitioner of the art and science of national liberation and self-defense, Brother Mao Tse-tung, put it this way: "We are advocates of the abolition of war, we do not want war; but war can only be abolished through war, and in order to get rid of the gun it is necessary to take up the gun."

The blood, sweat, tears and suffering of Black people are the foundations of the wealth and power of the United States of America. We were forced to build America, and if forced to, we will tear it down. The immediate result of this destruction will be suffering and bloodshed. But the end result will be the perpetual peace for all mankind.

Historically the power structure has demanded that Black leaders cater to their desires and to the ends of the imperialistic racism of the oppressor. The power structure has endorsed those Black leaders who have reduced themselves to nothing more than apologizing parrots. They have divided the so-called Black leaders within the political arena. The oppressors sponsor radio programs, give space in their racist newspapers, and show them the luxury enjoyed only by the oppressor. The Black leaders serve the oppressor by purposely keeping the people submissive, passive and non-violent, turning a deaf ear to the cries of the suffering and downtrodden, the unemployed and welfare recipients who hunger for liberation by any means necessary.

Historically there have been a few Black men who have rejected the handouts of the oppressor and who have refused to spread the oppressor's treacherous principles of deceit, gradual indoctrination and brainwashing, and who have refused to indulge in the criminal activity of teaching submission, fear, and love for an enemy who hates the very color Black and is determined to commit genocide on an international scale.

There has always existed in the Black colony of Afro-America a fundamental difference over which tactics, from the broad spectrum of alternatives, Black people should employ in their struggle for national liberation.

One side contends that Black people are in the peculiar position where, in order to gain acceptance into the "mainstream" of American life, they must employ no tactic that will anger the oppressor Whites. This view holds that Black people constitute a hopeless minority and that salvation for Black people lies in developing brotherly relations. There are certain tactics that are taboo. Violence against the oppressor must be avoided at all costs because the oppressor will retaliate with superior violence. So Black people may protest, but not protect. They can complain, but not cut and shoot. In short, Black people must at all costs remain non-violent.

On the other side we find that the point of departure is the principle that the oppressor has no rights that the oppressed is bound to respect. Kill the slavemaster, destroy him utterly, move against him with implacable fortitude. Break his oppressive power by any means necessary. Men who have stood before the Black masses and recommended this response to the oppression have been held in fear by the oppressor. The Blacks in the colony who were wed to the non-violent alternative could not relate to the advocates of implacable opposition to the oppressor. Because the oppressor always prefers to deal with the less radical, i.e., less dangerous spokesmen for his subjects. He would prefer that his subjects had no spokesmen at all, or better yet, he wishes to speak for them himself. Unable to do this practically, he does the next best thing and endorses spokesmen who will allow him to speak through them to the masses. Paramount among his imperatives is to see to it that implacable spokesmen are never allowed to communicate their message to the masses. Their oppressor will resort to any means necessary to silence them.

The oppressor, the "endorsed spokesmen," and the implacables form the three points of a triangle of death. The oppressor looks upon the endorsed spokesmen as a tool to use against the implacables to keep the masses passive within the acceptable limits of the tactics he is capable of containing. The endorsed spokesmen look upon the oppressor as a guardian angel who can always be depended upon to protect him from the wrath of the implacables, while he looks upon the implacables as dangerous and irresponsible madmen who, by angering the oppressor, will certainly provoke a blood bath in which they themselves might get washed away. The implacables view both the oppressors and the endorsed leaders as his deadly enemies. If anything, he has a more profound hatred for the endorsed leaders than he has for the oppressor himself, because the implacables know that they can deal with the oppressor only after they have driven the endorsed spokesmen off the scene.

Historically the endorsed spokesmen have always held the upper hand over the implacables. In Afro-American history there are shining brief moments when the implacables have outmaneuvered the oppressor and the endorsed spokesmen and gained the attention of the Black masses. The Black masses, recognizing the implacables in the depths of their despair, respond magnetically to the implacables and bestow a devotion and loyalty to them that frightens the oppressor and endorsed spokesmen into a panic-stricken frenzy, often causing them to leap into a rash act—murder, imprisonment, or exile—to silence the implacables and to get their show back on the road.

The masses of Black people have always been deeply entrenched and involved in the basic necessities of life. They have not had time to abstract their situation. Abstractions come only with leisure, the people have not had the luxury of leisure. Therefore, the people have been very aware of the true definition of politics. Politics is merely the desire of individuals and groups to satisfy their basic needs first: food, shelter and clothing, and security for themselves and their loved ones. The Black leaders endorsed by the power structure have attempted to sell the people the simple-minded theory that politics is holding a political office; being able to move into a $40,000 home; being able to sit near White people in a restaurant (while in fact the Black masses have not been able to pay the rent of a $40.00 rat-infested hovel).

The Black leaders have led the community to believe that brutality and force could be ended by subjecting the people to this very force of self-sacrificing demonstrations. The Black people realize brutality and force can only be inflicted if there is submission. The community has not responded in the past or in the present to the absurd, erroneous and deceitful tactics of so-called legitimate Black leaders. The community realizes that force and brutality can only be eliminated by counterforce through self-defense. Leaders who have recommended these tactics have never had the support and following of the downtrodden Black masses who comprise the bulk of the community. The grass roots, the downtrodden of the Black community, though rejecting the hand-picked "handkerchief heads" endorsed by the power structure, have not had the academic or administrative knowledge to form a long resistance to the brutality.

Marcus Garvey and Malcolm X were the two Black men of the twentieth century who posed an implacable challenge to both the oppressor and the endorsed spokesmen.

In our time, Malcolm stood on the threshold with the oppressor and the endorsed spokesmen in a bag that they could not get out of. Malcolm, implacable to the ultimate degree, held out to the Black masses the historical, stupendous victory of Black collective salvation and liberation from the chains of the oppressor and the treacherous embrace of the endorsed spokesmen. Only with the gun were the Black masses denied this victory. But they learned from Malcolm that with the gun they can recapture their dreams and make them a reality.

The heirs of Malcolm now stand millions strong on their corner of the triangle, facing the racist dog oppressor and the soulless endorsed spokesmen. The heirs of Malcolm have picked up the gun and taking first things first are moving to expose the endorsed spokesmen so the Black masses can see them for what they are and have always been. The choice offered by the heirs of Malcolm to the endorsed spokesmen is to repudiate the oppressor and to crawl back to their own people and earn a speedy reprieve or face a merciless, speedy and most timely execution for treason and being "too wrong for too long."

To the Black Movement:
May 15, 1968

QUESTION: The question of nationalism is a vital one in the Black movement today. Some have made a distinction between cultural nationalism and revolutionary nationalism. Would you comment on the differences and give us your views?

NEWTON: There are two kinds of nationalism: revolutionary nationalism and reactionary nationalism. Revolutionary nationalism is a people's revolution with the people in power as its goal. Therefore, to be a revolutionary nationalist you of necessity have to be a socialist. If you are a reactionary nationalist you are not a socialist and the consequences of your reactionary stance is the oppression of the people.

Cultural nationalism, or pork-chop nationalism as I sometimes call it, is basically a problem of having the wrong political perspective. It seems to be a reaction to, instead of an action against, political oppression. The cultural nationalists are concerned with returning to the old African culture and thereby regaining their identity and freedom. In other words, they feel that assuming the African culture is enough to bring political freedom. Many cultural nationalists fall into line as reactionary nationalists.

Papa Doc in Haiti is an excellent example of reactionary nationalism. He promotes the African culture while he oppresses the people. He's against anything non-Black, which on the surface seems very good. But in fact he is misleading the people. He merely kicked out the racists to replace them with himself as the oppressor. Many of the nationalists in this country seem to desire the same ends.

The Black Panther Party, which is a revolutionary group of Black people, realizes that we have to have an identity. We have to realize our Black heritage in order to give us strength to move on and progress. But as far as returning to the old African culture, it's unnecessary and in many respects unadvantageous. We believe that culture alone will not liberate us. We're going to need some stronger stuff.

A good example of revolutionary nationalism was the revolution in Algeria when Ben Bella took over. The French were kicked out, but because it was a people's revolution the people ended up in power. The leaders that took over were not interested in the profit motive or exploiting the people to keep them in slavery. They nationalized the industry and plowed the would-be profits back into the community. That's what socialism is all about. The people's representatives are in office strictly by the consent of the people. The wealth of the country is controlled by the people and they are considered whenever modifications in the industries are made.

The Black Panther Party is a revolutionary nationalist group and we see a major contradiction between capitalism in this country and our interests. We realize that this country became very rich upon slavery and that slavery is capitalism in the extreme. We have two evils to fight—capitalism and racism. We must destroy both racism and capitalism.

QUESTION: Directly related to the question of nationalism is the question of unity within the Black community. There has been some question about this since the Black Panther Party has run candidates against other Black candidates in recent California elections. What is your position on this matter?

NEWTON: Well, a very peculiar thing has happened. Historically you got what Malcolm X calls the field nigger and the house nigger. The house nigger had a few more privileges. He got the worn-out clothes of the master and he didn't have to work as hard as the field Black. He came to respect the master to the extent of identifying with him because he got a few of the leftovers that the field Blacks did not get. And through this identity with him he saw the slavemaster's interest as being his interest. Sometimes he would even protect the slavemaster more than the slavemaster would protect himself. Malcolm made the point that if the master's house happened to catch on fire the house Negro would work harder than the master to put the fire out and save the house. While the field Negro, the field Blacks, were praying that the house burned down. The house Black identified with the master so much that when the master would get sick the house Negro would say, "Master *we's* sick!"

The Black Panther Party are the field Blacks. We're hoping the master dies if he gets sick. The Black bourgeoisie seem to be acting out the role of the house Negro. They are pro-administration. They would like a few concessions made, but as far as the overall setup they have a little more material goods, a little more advantage, a few more privileges than the Black have-nots or the lower class. And so they identify with the power structure and they see their interests as the power structure's interest.

The Black Panther Party was forced to draw a line of demarcation. We are for all those who are for the promotion of the interests of the Black have-nots, who represent about 98 percent of Blacks here in America. We're not controlled by the White mother-country radical, nor are we controlled by the Black bourgeoisie. We have a mind of our own and if the Black bourgeoisie cannot align itself with our complete program, then the Black bourgeoisie sets itself up as our enemy. And they will be attacked and treated as such.

QUESTION: The Black Panther Party has had considerable

contact with White radicals since its earliest days. What do you see as the role of these White radicals?

NEWTON: The White mother-country radical is the offspring of the children of the beast that has plundered the world and exploited all people of color. These are children of the beast that seek now to be redeemed because they realize that their former heroes, who were slavemasters and murderers, put forth ideas that were only façades to hide the treachery they inflicted upon the world. They are turning their backs on their fathers.

The White mother-country radical, in resisting the system, becomes somewhat of an abstract thing because he is not oppressed as much as Black people are. As a matter of fact, his oppression is somewhat abstract simply because he doesn't have to live in a reality of oppression.

Black people in America and colored people throughout the world suffer not only from exploitation, but they suffer from racism. Black people here in America, in the Black colony, are oppressed because we're Black and we're exploited. The Whites are rebels, many of them are from the middle class and as far as any overt oppression, they have not experienced it. So therefore I call their rejection of the system somewhat of an abstract thing. They're looking for new heroes. They're looking to wash away the hypocrisy that their fathers have presented to the world. In doing this they see the people who are really fighting for freedom. They see the people who are really standing for justice and equality and peace throughout the world. These are the people of Vietnam, the people of Latin America, the people of Asia, the people of Africa, and the Black people in the Black colony here in America.

To the Republic of New Africa:
September 13, 1969*

Greetings to the Republic of New Africa and President Robert Williams. I'm very happy to be able to welcome you back home. I might add that this is perfect timing. We need you very much, the people need you very much. And now that the consciousness of the people is at such a high level, perhaps they will be able to appreciate your leadership, and also be ready to move in a very revolutionary fashion.

Some time ago I received a message from the Republic of New Africa with a series of questions concerning the philosophy of the Black Panther Party. At that time I wasn't prepared to send a message out. I have had to think about many of the questions, and due to the situation here it is very difficult for me to communicate, so this explains the lapse in time between question and answer. I will not be able to expound on all the questions but I would like to give some general explanations of the Black Panther Party's position as related to the Republic of New Africa.

The Black Panther Party's position is that the Black people in this country are definitely colonized, and suffer from the colonial plight more than any ethnic group in the country. Perhaps there is the exception of the Indian, but surely as much even as the Indian population. We, too, realize that the American people in general are colonized. And they are colonized simply because they are under a

* The Republic of New Africa, a separatist organization which advocates the establishment of a Black nation to be located in several Southern states in the U.S. Robert Williams is its President.

capitalist society which has a small clique of rulers who own the means of production and control all decision making. They are the body, therefore, that takes the freedom from the American people in general to enrich their own class. As far as Blacks are concerned, of course, we are at the very bottom of this ladder. We are exploited not only by the small group of the ruling class, we are oppressed and re-pressed by even the working-class Whites in the country. This is simply because the ruling class, the White ruling class, uses the old Roman policy of divide and conquer. In other words, the White working class is used as pawns or tools of the ruling class, but they too are enslaved. So it is with that historical policy of dividing and ruling that the ruling class can effectively and successfully keep the major-ity of the people in an oppressed position. This is because they are divided in certain interest groups, even though these "interests" of the lower-class groups are not neces-sarily of any real benefit to them.

As far as our stand on separation, we have demanded, as you well know, a plebiscite that the U.N. is to supervise, so that Blacks can decide whether they want to secede from the union or take another position. As far as the Black Panther Party is concerned we are subject to the will of the majority of the people, but we feel that the people should have this choice, and we feel that the Republic of New Africa is perfectly justified in demanding and declaring the right to secede from the union. So we don't have any contradiction between the Black Panther Party's position and the Republic of New Africa's position; it is simply a matter of timing. We feel that certain conditions will have to exist before we are even given the right to make that choice. We also take into consideration the fact that if Blacks at this very minute were able to secede from the union, and say have five or six states, it would be almost impossible to function in freedom side by side with a capitalist imperialistic country. We all know that Mother Africa is not free simply because of imperialism, because of Western domination. And there is no indication that it would be any different if we were to have a separate country here in North America. As a matter of fact, by all logics, we would suffer imperialism and colonialism even more so than the Third World is suffering it now. They are geographically better located, thousands of miles away, but yet they are not able to be free simply because of high technological development of the West that makes the world so much smaller, in fact, one small neighborhood.

So taking all these things into consideration, we conclude that the only way that we are going to be free is to wipe out once and for all the oppressive structure of America. We realize we cannot do this without a popular struggle, without many alliances and coalitions, and this is the reason that we are moving in the direction that we are, to get as many alliances as possible of people that are equally dissatisfied with the system. Also we are carrying on, or attempting to carry on, a political education campaign so that the people will be aware of the conditions and learn ways to control these conditions. We think that the most important thing at this time is to be able to organize in some fashion so that we will have a formidable force to challenge the structure of the American empire. So we invite the Republic of New Africa to struggle with us, because we know from people with whom I have talked (May Mallory, and other people who are familiar with the philosophy of the Republic of New Africa) that they seem to be very aware that the whole structure of America will have to be changed in order for the people of America to be free. (And this again is with the full knowledge and the full view of the end goal of the Republic of New Africa to secede.) In other words, we are not really handling the question at this time because we feel that it is somewhat premature, though I realize the psychological value of fighting for a territory. But at this time the Black Panther Party feels that we do not want to be in an enclave-type situation where we would be more isolated than we already are now. We are isolated in the ghetto area, concentrated in the North, in the metropolitan areas, in the industrial areas, and we think this is a very good location as far as strategy is concerned in waging a strong battle against the established order. And again I think that it would be perfectly justified if Blacks decided that they wanted to secede from the union, but I think the question should be left up to the popular masses, the popular majority. So this is it in a nutshell.

As I said before, I don't have the facilities here to carry on long discussions. I look forward to talking with Milton Henry in the near future if it is possible (I know that he has his hands full now) or representatives of the Republic of New Africa. There are many things I heard, things I read, that I'm in total agreement with. I would like for the Republic of New Africa to know that we support Robert Williams and his plight at this time; that we support him one hundred percent, and we're willing to give all services asked of us. Also we would like to find out exactly what we can do to be most helpful in the court proceedings coming up, what moral support we could give. Perhaps we could send some representatives; and we will publish in our paper, *The Black Panther,* the criminal activities that he has been victim of for some eight or nine years. I would also like to request of the Republic of New Africa to give us some support for Bobby Seale, our Chairman of the Black Panther Party. Bobby Seale is now in prison, as you know, in San Francisco. He has a case coming up in Chicago, and one in Connecticut, and we invite the Republic of New Africa to come in support. We would like this very much, and whatever moral support they could possibly give, we would welcome.

We should be working closer together than we are and perhaps this would be an issue that we could work together on. This issue is the political prisoners of America. And since people as one stand for the release of all political prisoners, this might be a rallying point for all of the Black revolutionary organizations and parties. Because I truly believe that some good comes out of every attack that the oppressor makes, and this will be a turning point in both of our organizations and parties. So I would like to say, "ALL POWER TO THE PEOPLE, AND MORE POWER TO THE PRESIDENT OF THE REPUBLIC OF NEW AFRICA, ROBERT WILLIAMS."

Black Capitalism Re-Analyzed I:
June 5, 1971

This is a dialogue in our continuing discussion of the new thrust of the Black Panther Party, as we begin to carry out the original vision of the Party. When we coined the expression "All Power to the People," we had in mind emphasizing the word "Power," for we recognize that the *will to power is the basic drive of man*. But it is incorrect to seek power over people. We have been subjected to the dehumanizing power of exploitation and racism for hundreds of years; and the Black community has its own will to power also. What we seek, however, is not power over people, but the power to control our own destiny. For us the true definition of power is not in terms of how many people you can control. To us power is the ability to first of all define phenomena, and secondly the ability to make these phenomena act in a desired manner.

We see then that power has a dual character and that we cannot simply identify and define phenomena without acting, for to do so is to become an armchair philosopher. And when Bobby and I left Merritt College to organize brothers on the block we did so because the college students were too content to sit around and analyze without acting. On the other hand, power includes action, for it is making phenomena perform in the desired manner. But action without thinking and theory is also incorrect, for if the social forces at work in the community have not been correctly analyzed and defined how can you control them in such a way that they act in a desired manner? So the Black

Panther Party has always merged theory and practice in such a way as to serve the true interests of the community.

In merging theory with practice we recognized that it was necessary to develop a theory which was valid for more than *one* time and place. We wanted to develop a system of thinking which was good anywhere, thus it had to be rather abstract. Yet our theory would relate to a concrete analysis of concrete conditions so that our actions would always be relevant and profitable to the people. Yet, at the same time, it had to advance their thinking so that they would move toward a transformation of their situation of exploitation and oppression. We have always insisted on good theory and good practice, but we have not always been successful in carrying this through.

When the Black Panther Party defected from the Black community, we became, for a while, revolutionary cultists. One of the primary characteristics of a revolutionary cultist is that he despises everyone who has not reached his level of consciousness, or the level of consciousness that he thinks he has reached, instead of acting to bring the people to that level. In that way the revolutionary cultist becomes divided from the people; he defects from the community. Instead of serving the people as a vanguard, he becomes a hero. Heroes engage in very courageous actions sometimes and they often make great sacrifices, including the supreme sacrifice, but they are still isolated from the people. Their courageous actions and sacrifices do not lead the people to a higher level of consciousness, nor do they produce fundamental changes in the exploitation and oppression of the people. A vanguard, however, will guide the people onto higher levels of consciousness and in that way bring them to the point where they will take sterner actions in their own interests and against those who continue to oppress them. As I've said previously, revolution is a process, not a conclusion. A true revolutionist will not only take courageous actions, he will also try to advance the people in such a manner that they will transform their situation. That is, by delivering power to the people the true revolutionist will help them define the social phenomena in their community and lead them to the point where they will seize the time and make these phenomena act in a desired manner.

Therefore, as revolutionaries we must recognize the difference between what the people can do and what they will do. They can do anything they desire to do, but they will only take those actions which are consistent with their level of consciousness and their understanding of the situation. When we raise their consciousness, they will understand even more fully what they in fact can do, and they will move on the situation in a courageous manner. This is merging your theory with your practices.

Point 3 of the original Ten-Point Program of the Black Panther Party is "We want an end to the robbery by the CAPITALISTS of our Black Community." *That was our position in October 1966 and it is still our position.* We recognize that capitalism is no solution to the problems we face in our communities. Capitalist exploitation is one of the basic causes of our problem. It is the goal of the Black Panther Party to negate capitalism in our communities and in the oppressed communities throughout the world.

However, many people have offered the community Black capitalism as a solution to our problems. We recognize that people in the Black community have no general dislike for the concept of Black capitalism, but this is not because they are in love with capitalism. Not at all. The idea of Black capitalism has come to mean to many people Black control of another one of the institutions in the community. We see within this characteristic the seeds of the negation of Black capitalism and all capitalism in general. What we must do then is increase the positive qualities until they dominate the negative and therefore transform the situation.

In the past the Black Panther Party took a counterrevolutionary position with our blanket condemnation of Black capitalism. Our strategy should have been to analyze the positive and negative qualities of this phenomenon before making any condemnation. Even though we recognized, and correctly so, that capitalism is no solution or answer, we did not make a truly dialectical analysis of the situation.

We recognized that in order to bring the people to the level of consciousness where they would seize the time, it would be necessary to serve their interests in survival by developing programs which would help them to meet their daily needs. For a long time we have had such programs not only for survival but for organizational purposes. Now we not only have a breakfast program for schoolchildren, we have clothing programs, we have health clinics which provide free medical and dental services, we have programs for prisoners and their families, and we are opening clothing and shoe factories to provide for more of the needs of the community. Most recently we have begun a testing and research program on sickle-cell anemia, and we know that 98 percent of the victims of this disease are Black. To fail to combat this disease is to submit to genocide; to battle it is survival.

All these programs satisfy the deep needs of the community but they are not solutions to our problems. That is why we call them survival programs, meaning survival pending revolution. We say that the survival program of the Black Panther Party is like the survival kit of a sailor stranded on a raft. It helps him to sustain himself until he can get completely out of that situation. So the survival programs are not answers or solutions, but they will help us to organize the community around a true analysis and understanding of their situation. When consciousness and understanding is raised to a high level then the community will seize the time and deliver themselves from the boot of their oppressors.

All our survival programs are free. We have never

charged the community a dime to receive the things they
need from any of our programs and we will not do so. We
will not get caught up in a lot of embarrassing questions or
paperwork which alienate the people. If they have a need
we will serve their needs and attempt to get them to understand the true reasons why they are in need in such an
incredibly rich land. Survival programs will always be operated without charge to those who need them and benefit by
them.

In order to carry out such programs we have always
needed money. In the past we received money from wealthy
White philanthropists, humanitarians, and heirs to the corporate monopolies. At the same time we were engaging in
a blanket condemnation of the small victimized Black capitalists found in our communities. This tactic was wrong
since we receive the money for our survival programs from
big White capitalists, and we freely admit that.

When we say that we see within Black capitalism the
seeds of its own negation and the negation of all capitalism,
we recognize that the small Black capitalist in our communities has the potential to contribute to the building of the
machine which will serve the true interests of the people
and end all exploitation. By increasing the positive qualities
of the Black capitalist we may be able to bring about a non-
antagonistic solution of his contradiction with the community, while at the same time heightening the oppressed
community's contradiction with the large corporate capitalist empire. This will intensify the antagonistic contradiction between the oppressed community and the empire; and
by heightening that contradiction there will subsequently
be a violent transformation of the corporate empire. We will
do this through our survival programs which have the
interest of the community at heart.

We now see the Black capitalist as having a similar
relationship to the Black community as the national
(native) bourgeoisie have to the people in national wars of

decolonization. In wars of decolonization the national bourgeoisie supports the freedom struggle of the people because they recognize that it is in their own selfish interest. Then when the foreign exploiter has been kicked out, the national bourgeoisie takes his place and continues the exploitation. However, the national bourgeoisie is a weaker group even though they are exploiters.*

Since the people see Black capitalism in the community as Black control of local institutions, this is a positive characteristic because the people can bring more direction and focus to the activities of the capitalist. At the same time the Black capitalist who has the interest of the community at heart will respond to the needs of the people because this is where his true strength lies. So far as capitalism in general is concerned, the Black capitalist merely has the status of a victim because the big White capitalists have the skills, make the loans, and in fact control the Black capitalist. If he wants to succeed in his enterprise the Black capitalist must turn to the community because he depends on them to make his profits. He needs this strong community support because he cannot become independent of the control of the corporate capitalists who control the large monopolies.

The Black capitalist will be able to support the people by contributing to the survival programs of the Black Panther Party. In contributing to such programs he will be able to help build the vehicle which will eventually liberate the Black community. He will not be able to deliver the people from their problems, but he will be able to help build the strong political machine which will serve as a revolutionary vanguard and guide the people in their move toward freedom.

---

* Presently the bourgeoisie is in a weaker position now than it was when it was freed from colonialism. Under Reactionary Intercommunalism (such as in Europe) the bourgeoisie is in control of a smaller unit (community) than it was before. Not only does this make it weaker, it also makes a non-antagonistic transformation of their contradiction more likely since the objective interests of the bourgeoisie are in many ways similar to the interests of poor people. (H. P. N.)

Poster of Huey P. Newton in window of former Black Panther Headquarters in Oakland, after being shot up by police

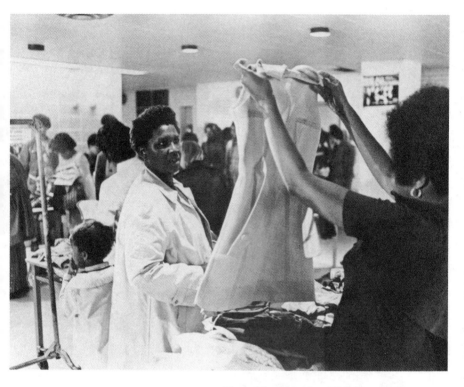

Free Clothing for Children Rally,
P.S. 201 Harlem

Free Food and Shoe Program,
West Oakland, California

Free Breakfast Program,
West Oakland, California

Free Breakfast Program,
Berkeley, California

Free Shoe Program, Richmond, California

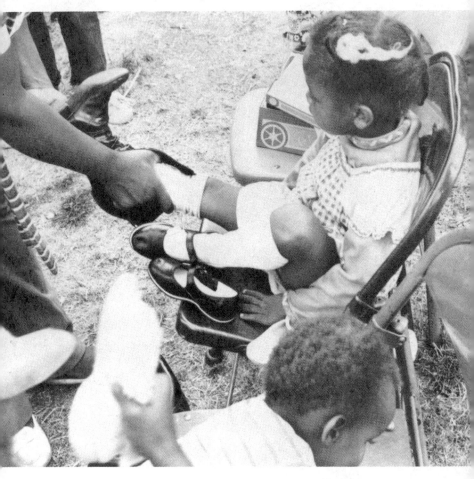

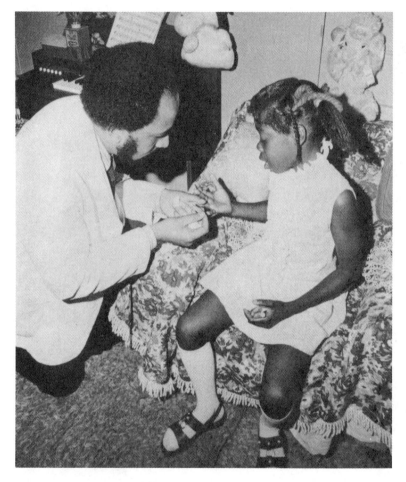

People's Free Health Clinic—Sickle Cell Anemia Program, Rox-
bury, Massachusetts

Press conference held at end of Cal-Pak Boycott. From left to right, Bill Boyette, Huey P. Newton, Congressman Ron Dellums. (Photo by Tim Sowell, Jr.)

Huey P. Newton and Premier Chou En-lai

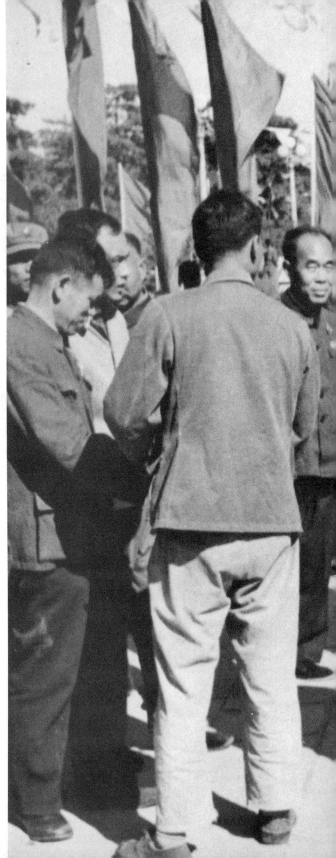

Huey Newton
and other
Panthers at
National Day
Celebrations,
October,
1971, Peking

On grounds of National Minorities Institute, Peking

At nursery of locomotive parts factory near Peking

At nursery
of locomotive parts
factory near Peking

Huey P. Newton and President of FRELIMO (Front for the
Liberation of Mozambique) Samora Moises Machel

Our re-analysis of Black capitalism and its relationship to the community from the perspective of dialectical materialism, and our practical understanding of the needs of the community and the attitudes of the people toward Black capitalism, leads us to a new position. Black businesses which have the interests of the community at heart will be able to contribute to the people through the community programs of the Black Panther Party. These free programs will help the community to survive and thus deter the genocide which is always a threat to our existence here.

In return for these contributions the Black Panther Party will carry advertisements of these businesses in our paper and urge the community to support them. We will never sell advertising space in the paper, but we will give space in return for contributions to the survival programs which are given free to the community. In this way we will achieve a greater unity of the community of victims—the people who are victimized by the society in general, and the Black capitalists who are victimized by the corporate capitalist monopolies. In this way we will increase the positive qualities of Black capitalism until they dominate the negative qualities, and exploitation will no longer be the reality which the community reluctantly accepts.

The community will see those who support their survival and patronize their places of business. At the same time the community will also criticize those who refuse to participate in their survival programs, and turn their backs on them. If the establishment tries to come down hard on those businessmen who support the survival programs, then the community will recognize this as another form of oppression and will move to strongly defend their supporters. In that way the consciousness of the people and the level of the struggle will be advanced.

There is no salvation in capitalism, but through this new approach the Black capitalist will contribute to his own negation by helping to build a strong political vehicle which is guided by revolutionary concepts and serves as a vanguard for the people. In a way our new position has the simplicity and completeness of a mathematical formula. When the Black capitalist contributes to the survival programs and makes a contribution to the community, the community will give him their support and thus strengthen his business. If he does not make any contribution to the survival of the community the people will not support him and his enterprise will wither away because of his own negligence. By supporting the community, however, he will be helping to build the political machine which will eventually negate his exploitation of the community, but also negate his being exploited and victimized by corporate capitalism.

So we will heighten the contradiction between the Black community and corporate capitalism, while at the same time reducing the contradiction between the Black capitalist and the Black community. In this way Black capitalism will be transformed from a relationship of exploitation of the community to a relationship of service to the community, which will contribute to the survival of everyone.

Black Capitalism Re-Analyzed II
(*Practical Application*):
August 9, 1971

We recently participated in boycotting Mayfair Supermarket.* Mayfair (located at 61st and Telegraph Avenue in Oakland, California), is located in the Black community, but had the audacity to purchase alcoholic beverages from companies that excluded Black truckdrivers. The California State Package Store and Tavern Owners Association (an organization of Black-owned small retail liquor stores and taverns) initiated the boycott of Mayfair and the Black Panther Party joined them. We closed Mayfair in four days.

The major businesses of Blacks are liquor stores, taverns, mortuaries, realty, barber shops, beauty parlors and barbeque pits: victims all with concomitant positive and negative qualities. The Black Panther Party is a community-wide intercommunal force. We want to organize Black busi-

* The boycott was successfully resolved in January, 1972. The press release by Ron Dellums, who helped negotiate the settlement, said in part, "We are announcing today that an agreement has been reached of great importance to all of the people in the Bay Area and, in particular, the Black population of this area. This agreement, between the Black Panther Party and the Ad Hoc Committee for Promotion of Black Business, officially ends the boycott of Boyette's Liquor Stores by the Black Panther Party . . . The United Fund of the Bay Area, Inc., sponsored and created by the Ad Hoc Committee for the Promotion of Black Business and the Cal-Pak Liquor Dealers, has already begun the task of collecting funds from Black businesses and individuals for programs of special need in the Black community. Operating as a non-profit social vehicle for the Black community, this new organization will make disbursements to various significant organizations in the Black community on a regular and continuing basis. Among the programs that will benefit are the survival programs of the Black Panther Party.

nesses so that while making a living themselves they may also serve the Black community that gives them their small profits. We want them united. We want them to act in unison. We want them to use a common bank in order to give themselves more economic muscle. If they are strong they can better serve the Black community. Why then, you may ask, is Cal-Pak now a boycott target? We feel that we must organize the family first so that we may go out and seek that which is due the family. In order to do this we must build a solid foundation through a community-focused Black united front. We cannot afford the luxury of "individualism." The idea of Black individualism is sheer madness, impotence personified. The Black Panther Party has community survival programs that must have the support of those who are able to help. Support of these survival programs will build a strong Black community.

In order to unite the Black community and in order to establish a positive, complementary economic linkage between the completely destitute and those who have a few pennies, we will first persuade through petition then through the boycott when necessary. We see very little difference between Blacks who make profits from the Black community and refuse to contribute to Black survival programs, and the White profiteers such as Mayfair. We only ask a nominal continuing contribution from Cal-Pak as a group. They may set the amount, but we feel they must contribute something on a continuing predictable basis as long as the need exists. We do not want Black businessmen to go out of business, which is why they and no one else must decide what they are able to contribute to survival programs. If they go out of business they cannot help the Black community. But if they refuse to help the Black community they are parasites that must be forced out of business through economic boycott. Why should the Black community nourish a Black profiteer who has no concern for his brother?

During the latter part of June, 1971, the Black Panther Party held a series of meetings with Cal-Pak Package Store and Tavern Owners Association and asked their continuing, voluntary, self-determined (in terms of amount) support of survival programs. After a series of meetings Cal-Pak was steadfast in a single offer of bread, milk, meat and eggs for the free breakfast program. They said they would not contribute on a continuing basis. They wanted to make a pay-off, which we rejected. We are not extortionists.

We explained that a continuing trickle of support is more important to the community than a large, once-only hush-mouth gift. We will not be paid off; we will not be quiet; we will not go away as long as there is one hungry child, one barefoot person, one medically neglected individual, or one brother or sister without a winter coat.

Mr. Bill Boyette is the President of California-State Package Store and Tavern Owners Association. He has two liquor stores, one at 25th and Grove Street, the other at 54th and Grove Street. We ask you not to shop at these stores. Mr. Boyette has given no positive leadership to Cal-Pak; he has been negativistic and has suppressed those members of Cal-Pak who are now and have been support-ing survival programs as individual businessmen. They have not been able to contribute through Cal-Pak because Mr. Boyette and other parasites in Cal-Pak have refused to allow participation through a united front.

Please do not shop at Bill's Liquor Stores on Grove at 25th Street, and Grove at 54th Street! We invite all com-munity people to come out and join the picket line at 54th and Grove Street between 6 A.M. and 2 A.M. daily. Come and stay a few minutes or as long as you wish. It is our united duty to build a strong community. We will continue the boycott until Mr. Boyette changes his mind.

HE WON'T BLEED ME
A Revolutionary Analysis of Sweet Sweetback's Baadasssss Song
With an Introduction by Bobby Seale, June 19, 1971

The feeling that I have now that I am back on the scene with Brother Huey P. Newton is one where I remember the times when Brother Huey was always there to interpret the cultural things and symbolic forms and expressions of the people in different forms of art. This was over three and a half years ago, the last time Brother Huey and I were together.

Now that I am back on the scene I have had the chance to be with many righteous Party members and community people. Together we have shared the experience of going to the theater to see Sweet Sweetback, *the latest movie on the set. Our Minister of Defense, righteous, beautiful Brother Huey P. Newton was there interpreting all the symbolic meanings of the movie, and showing the essence of the real-life experience of the Black community as it is put together in* Sweet Sweetback.

Brother Huey P. Newton is free, and we are both out in the larger social prison; but we are with our people in the Black community and Brother Huey P. Newton is giving a beautiful revolutionary people's analysis of Sweet Sweetback.

When we have read the analysis given by Brother Huey we should unite as brothers and sisters in the struggle and go back and see Sweet Sweetback *not to be entertained but because we can be educated and our consciousness and understanding can be increased. I am going to see it again with Brother Huey's analysis as my guide. I hope you will too.*

Bobby Seale

The very popular movie produced and directed by Melvin Van Peebles called *Sweet Sweetback's Baadasssss Song* contains many very important messages for the entire Black community. On many levels Van Peebles is attempting to communicate some crucial ideas, motivating us to a deeper understanding and then action based upon that understanding. He has certainly made effective use of one of the most popular forms of communication, the movie, and he is dealing in revolutionary terms. The only reason this movie is available to us with its many messages is because Black people have given it their highest support. The corporate capitalist would never let such an important message be given to the community if they were not so greedy. They are so anxious to bleed us for more profits that they either ignore or fail to recognize the many ideas in the film. And because we have supported the movie with our attendance we are able to receive its message.

It is the first truly revolutionary Black film made and it is presented to us by a Black man. Many Black people who have seen the film have missed many of its significant points. I have seen the film several times and I have also talked to about fifty to sixty others who have seen it and each time I understand more.

When Van Peebles first presented the film he refused to submit it to the Motion Picture Association to be rated because he knew they were not competent to judge its content. He knew the film was not something which would upset the Black community because of its explicitness. He wanted youth and children to see it because he knew they would understand it. Yet the movie was given an "X" rating over his protests, thus making it impossible for the youth to see. But it has a real message for them, for just like "Moo-Moo," one of the youthful characters in the movie, they are our future.

Melvin Van Peebles had great difficulty obtaining the funds to make this movie, therefore it has a low budget. In some parts the sound and the lighting are not as good as they might have been if he could have had more money to make the film. I have found that its messages and significance are clearer when I combine viewing the film with listening to the record of the sound track and reading the book. I would urge all of you who want to understand the deep meanings of the movie to also buy the record and the book.

Sweet Sweetback blows my mind every time I talk about it because it is so simple and yet so profound. It shows the robbery which takes place in the Black community and how we are the real victims. Then it shows how the victims must deal with their situation, using many institutions and many approaches. It demonstrates that one of the key routes to our survival and the success of our resistance is unity.

Sweet Sweetback does all of this by using many aspects of the community, but in symbolic terms. That is, Van Peebles is showing one thing on the screen but saying something more to the audience. In other words he is signifying, and he is signifying some very heavy things.

When the movie opens we see the faces of women; there are young faces and old faces, but in all of them there is a sign of weariness, sadness, but also joy. You soon recognize that the women are in a house of love, a house of prostitution, a house of ill-repute. Of course it can be any of these things, depending on what position you are viewing it from. This is the essence of the whole film, the victim and the oppressor looking at things in a much different way, from a different point of view.

The women are tired yet they are happy. This is because they are feeding a small boy. As you look at the women you see that they are strong and beautiful Black women, definitely African in ancestry and symbolic of Mother Africa. The size of some of their breasts signifies how Africa is potentially the breadbasket of the world. The women are feeding stew to a small boy who is apparently very hungry, and as he downs it they keep offering him more. These women with their large breasts potentially could feed and nourish the world, and if this is so, certainly they have the potential to raise their liberator, for that is what the small boy is, the future of the women, of Black people, liberation.

They are in a house of prostitution not of their own will, but because of the conditions the oppressor makes for us. They are there to survive and they sell their love to do so, therefore our love is distorted and corrupted with the sale. When you have nothing else left you give up your body, just as when you are starving you might eat your fingers; but it is the conditions which cause this, not the desire to taste your own blood; you have to survive.

The women standing around the small boy are not saying anything but by continuing to nourish him they are telling him that they can give him more than enough; not only food, but much love. This love is not for sale and is therefore uncorrupted. It is pure love, sacred and holy. Even though the boy is weak and has many sores on his face, with the love and nourishment of the women he can become a very strong man. The sores on his face come from malnutrition and poor health and Van Peebles is signifying the fine line between survival and death. Even though the women can feed him and clear up his malnutrition, they cannot do it freely and totally because they have to sell, also they have to sell in order to provide.

I have seen small children in the Brownsville section of Brooklyn, in West Oakland, in Chicago, and in Harlem with sores on their bodies like those on the boy's face. That is why we have health and food programs, because we are determined to make them healthy again. The women in the film are doing the same thing. They know he is their future and so they give him love and nourishment that he might become a strong man, not just in the physical sense, but so he might become a liberator.

Next we see the boy is healthy and growing, working as a towel boy in the house of prostitution. Then we see the prostitute making love to him. But this was a scene of pure love and therefore it was a sacred and holy act. Even though it was in a house of prostitution, it was not a distorted or corrupt thing. We see this by the very words the woman uses, for she tells the boy that he ain't at the photographer to get his picture taken; she tells him to move. In the background we hear religious music signifying what is happening and what will happen later. First there is "Wade in the Water," and we recognize that the boy is being baptized; then there is "This Little Light of Mine, I'm Gonna Let It Shine," signifying what will happen in the future. The music indicates that this is not a sexual scene, this is a very sacred rite. For the boy, who was nourished to health, is now being baptized into manhood; and the act of love, the giving of manhood, is also bestowing upon the boy the characteristics which will deliver him from very difficult situations. People who look upon this as a sex scene miss the point completely, and people who look upon the movie as a sex movie miss the entire message of the film.

What happens is not a distorted act of prostitution even though it takes place in a house of prostitution. The place is profane because of the oppressive conditions, but so are our communities also oppressed. The Black community is often profane because of the dirtiness there, but this is not caused by the people because they are the victims of a very oppressive system. Yet within the heart of the community, just as in the film, the sacred rite of feeding and nourishing the youth goes on; they are brought to their manhood as liberators.

Van Peebles shows this in the film because when the love scene is completed, the boy is no longer a boy; he has become a man. He doesn't have a climax until he reaches an adult age. Even though we may have sexual intercourse as children, we don't have a climax; it is an introduction which makes it a part of something which is not alien to us. But in the film the climax came at the appropriate time, after he has become a man. That is, he has learned the deep significance of what she was trying to teach him. It wasn't an act or any mechanical sort of thing, but it was the building of his spirit.

So he grows a mustache while he is having sexual intercourse with her, from about ten years old he ends up to be about twenty-five. But as soon as he reaches a climax, that is, as soon as he becomes a man, then he is ready to go out and fight. This is symbolized by his putting on his hat because when you put on your hat it symbolizes that you are fixing to go somewhere.

The whole film is centered around movement: his putting on the hat to go and his running and running. I think this shows the alienation he feels in his position. He is constantly in movement or "in the process." When you are in the process you are always going or preparing to go. These symbols are used very well.

The oppressor would not view the love scene in the same way because his whole introduction to sex is from a perverted perspective and divorced from his whole being. That is why he rated the film "X" because what he saw was a sex movie. We know that it is much more than that. He is introduced to sex as something outside of himself, while it is hard for us to remember our first sexual experience. It is not something outside of us, but it grows in us as any other part of our personality, and it is integrated into our physical selves just as our arms, our hands or our breathing is. This is why it was very necessary to show this young boy having this relationship in a place that is viewed from the outside as dirty and profane.

But we do love and we do have holy experiences at the same time that we are being stripped of everything else. Then we sell that holiness in order to survive, but it is not holiness any more, it is transformed by the sale. Nevertheless, the holiness is a part of us, so it serves us. But at the same time the holiness serves us it remains as dirtiness to the outsider because he is the cause of the profane conditions of the victims, and because what he is getting is not love, but the sale of the prostitute.

To the boy she was not a prostitute because there was no money passed. Instead she introduced him to the thing that would give him his fullness as a person and his survival in the end. She introduced it to him as a boy because it is said, "Train up a child in the way he should go: and when he is old, he will not depart from it." (Proverbs 22:6) Of course he won't depart from it if it becomes an integral part of his personality because he would be departing from himself. The women were giving the boy more than simply a survival thing because he was their hope, and this is why they feel happy about the sacrifice they are making. You can see it on their faces when they are feeding him and at the point of orgasm when the woman tells him that he has a sweet back, which is where he gets his name. Not only is he baptized into his fullness as a man, he gets his name and his identity in this sacred rite.

After that, whenever Sweetback engages in sex with a sister it is always an act of survival and a step towards his liberation. That is why it is important not to view the movie as a sex film or the sexual scenes as actual sex acts. Van Peebles is righteously signifying to us all. The first scene was far from being sexual, that is why holy music plays during the scene. It is only dealing with sexual symbols. The real meaning is far away from anything sexual, and so deep that you have to call it religious.

When Sweetback puts on his hat he does not leave the house, he does not leave the victim's ghettos, but graduates to perform there in a freak show. He would simulate sexual intercourse before an audience that paid to observe this scene. He starts out playing the part of a dyke, with false breasts and a beard, but then his "fairy godmother" comes along and he gets his wish and becomes a man before the audience, taking off his beard and showing his penis—it looks like a missile and shocks the audience.

While this is going on, the cops are harassing Beatle, who is the owner of the cat house. He has been paying them off and doesn't want to be bothered, but they want one of his men as a scapegoat arrest. The cops break off their harassment from time to time and go over to observe the freak show, even though they have seen it many times.

Sweetback is now having sexual intercourse with the sister, but there is no holy music because it is not love; it is a performance given in order to survive. He is selling himself to the audience and the cops, who are the freaks. Dylan's "Ballad of the Thin Man" would apply here, because in the song the freaks go to see the geek who offers them a bone and they don't know why. But you see the audience or the freaks—including the cops—don't have to be there. They cause the conditions which make it necessary for people to go to these lengths to survive and then they pay to see the performance the people put on. They are the real freaks and the people go through the act with real hostility and hatred for the people who cause them to be there in the first place.

There are also Blacks in the audience. This is a stroke of genius by Van Peebles because it symbolizes the total blindness of the audience of freaks. They are laughing at a situation when they are in fact getting their heads cut off. That's like Dylan's sword swallower, who in the end will thank the audience for the loan because they were really there, only they did not know it. The scene shows how far the oppressor will go, for when it is asked if anyone in the audience wants to challenge Sweetback, this White boy couldn't hold his girlfriend down. The announcer would not let her go out there because the police were watching.

The police, as I said, are taking payoffs and letting the house exist. This is an indictment of them. The freak show is not put on by freaks but by victims. The victim does what he has to do to survive because of his crippled and victimized position. The freak pays him for his laughter and the victim accepts the pay, but with vengeance in mind.

It is ironic and very symbolic that even while I am writing this I can look out of my window and see the Oakland Auditorium where the Oakland Police Officers Association is holding its annual circus. I don't see any Blacks going in. We are realizing more and more that it has always been a circus. They have tried to make a circus of our circumstances and our communities, but our awareness is growing and we are moving toward dealing with the situation in a very decisive manner, just like Sweet Sweetback did.

In the film and in the community the oppressor keeps demanding more and more from the victims—that is why they want one of Beatle's men. But this is also why the victim with the lowest level of awareness will be brought into consciousness and revolutionized because he is doing what he is doing in order to survive. But eventually his very survival is at stake. The oppressor won't even let your acts of survival continue; he tries to totally crush you until survival becomes a very revolutionary act. At the point of life and death, all of the hatred for the oppressor is unleashed for survival purposes.

The police in the film really don't want Sweetback. All they want to do is use him for a cover because they are going after Moo-Moo, the young revolutionary. Sweetback goes along with them because of his low level of consciousness. This is no hard task because when an individual victim acts without awareness of the situation, he is just like the organism that wants to survive. THE UNITY COMES OUT OF CONSCIOUSNESS.

For a short while Moo-Moo and Sweetback are handcuffed together, but when the police start to beat the life out of Moo-Moo, they separate them and tell Sweetback to stand aside. Sweetback attempts to look away from the beating.

This shows the arrogance of the aggressor, his Jehovah complex, thinking that he has all the control. He thinks that he has his victims so completely in line that this freak show performer, who is paying them so that he can survive, will have no feelings for another victim.

Sweetback attempts to look away while the police are beating Moo-Moo. Just the turning away shows how much of the time the masses attempt to dismiss the atrocities of the oppressor, even when attempts are made to communicate to them. They will pretend that they are too busy with other things because they are trying to survive; but they fail to realize that their real survival depends upon their social consciousness and therefore unity. The oppressor will demand more and more of them until they will perish without that unity.

At its lowest level, survival is just the organism getting by as an individual person or as an individual family. What they must realize is that the oppressor will not allow that, he will keep demanding more: high unemployment, poor housing, poor health and poor education, and more taxes, until that organism's very death. So they attempt to look away, but because of compassion and their identity with the whole situation they cannot completely turn their backs. This is what causes the neurosis of some Blacks.

Through Sweetback, Melvin Van Peebles is righteously signifying and teaching the people what must really be done to survive. When Sweetback realizes that he cannot turn his back, he takes the handcuffs, the chains which have been used to hold him in slavery, and he starts to kick ass. Using his handcuffs as a weapon against the oppressor rather than as the tool of submission, he downs both of the policemen, almost cutting off their heads.

This is a very bloody scene but it was very important that they showed the blood all the way up his arm. It makes me think of the statement by Frantz Fanon in *The Wretched of the Earth*, where he says that the peasant creeps into the settler's room at night and cracks the settler's head open.

Then the blood spurts across the peasant's face, and it is the only baptism he ever remembered.

The Black audiences really respond to this scene because it is another baptism; but instead of wading in the water as Sweetback did earlier, this is a baptism in blood. As each blow went down, you could hear the tension being released in the audience because right at that moment it was a climax for them.

One of the few criticisms I have of this film is that there is no religious music behind this scene. This is no more a scene of violence than the earlier baptism was one of sex; it is a growing into manhood. Sweetback grew into a man when he was in bed with that woman and he also grew to be a man when he busted the heads of his oppressors. When he was with the woman it was like a holy union, and when he takes the heads of his oppressors it is like taking the sacrament for the first time. In the first baptism he did not become a whole man because he went into that freak show, but when he is baptized in the blood he righteously moves on to a higher level because the next time he is with the police with handcuffs on, he gets away. And the time after that when he is with the police with handcuffs on, in that pool hall, he knows what he must do and he does it.

Like I said before, Van Peebles is righteously signifying because he engages the audience in a climax when Sweetback downs the police. What he does is equate the most ecstatic moments in the film with the actions he is encouraging the people to engage in. So he is advocating a bloody overthrow because the victims want to survive.

The next point that Van Peebles develops in the film is the need of the Black community for greater unity and how the lack of unity will only deliver us into the hands of our oppressors. What happens? Sweetback helps Moo-Moo get up, but then goes his own way and makes it back to the cat house where he encounters Beatle. Beatle starts to give him advice, but everybody recognizes that Beatle is not really responding to Sweetback's situation. Van Peebles gets this point across beautifully. While he is giving advice Beatle is sitting on the toilet. He wipes himself, gets up, and without washing his hands he takes a towel and wipes his face. This is signifying that what is coming out of Beatle's mouth is the same thing that is coming out the other end—shit and nothing else. Notice that Sweetback never says a word to Beatle, but he does not have to because Beatle is deaf and cannot hear what is being said anyway.

When he leaves Beatle, the camera shows Sweetback with a terrified look on his face. He has realized that those he knows best have such a low level of awareness that he cannot expect aid from them. He realizes that the lack of unity is a very hurting thing, and when he walks out of Beatle's place he walks right into the hands of the police, who pretend to be nice until they realize that he is not playing the part of the meek victim. Then they work him over thoroughly.

Sweetback is saved by that same unity he failed to find with Beatle. The people rescue him by pretending to be in need of money, and offer to wash the car of the police. Instead they are engaging in a very revolutionary act and save the brother from the oppressor while at the same time delivering a deadly blow to the police. What Sweetback has done for Moo-Moo is repeated for him by the community.

Sweetback is on his own now but he is locked into a pair of handcuffs. How does he get them off? Through unity. He goes to a woman, whom he has been with before, and she tells him to beg. This is obviously not the first time this has happened, but Sweetback cannot beg any more because he has been transformed by the baptism in blood. He needs her at this moment, but sexuality cannot be based on war any longer but on love and unity. He makes love to her and after that the handcuffs are off. This signifies that it is the unity between the Black man and the Black woman which is able to liberate them both.

In his first baptism Sweetback acquired the ability to love, but he could only truly love and unify with the woman when he had done away with the people who made his woman the oppressor's woman and himself the oppressor's man. Then they could really have unity which is symbolic of the liberating love of the Black man and woman.

Sweetback is on his own again, but this time without the handcuffs. In the meantime the film takes us back to the cat house and his old boss, Beatle. Beatle is being hassled by the police who want to know where to find Sweetback. Beatle doesn't really know, but if he did he would have told them because Beatle had no consciousness—he is deaf. And to prove how true this is, the police finally deafen him.

Sweetback moves through the community looking for the assistance he needs to get away. He doesn't get all that he needs, but he gets all that each can give. At the church he gets a Black Ave Maria and the power sign. The minister recognizes that his religion is a hype, for he tells Sweetback that Moo-Moo is giving the people the real religion.

At the gambling den he gets little apparent sympathy. The manager keeps telling him he is a dead man and he really does not need money. In this scene Van Peebles is again showing the community of the victimized, just like the performers in the freak show, because the manager explains to Sweetback that he cannot make any money on his operation. By the time he gets finished paying off everybody who is exploiting him, he pays a dollar and a dime for every dollar he makes. This is another example of the oppressor demanding more and more of the victims.

But the gambler does what he can—he gives Sweetback a ride. There is some unity, but not enough; and during the ride Sweetback spots Moo-Moo, the man he left behind, and they are reunited. This is as it should be, because Sweetback is leaving the community with the person who was the beginning of all this, Moo-Moo. They are two unlike characters yet they are linked together.

Moo-Moo symbolizes the revolutionary who is trying to free the people. His whole program is pointed toward people like Sweetback, community people who are very unaware yet trying to survive. Sweetback at this point symbolizes the most unconscious persons in the community, people who are sometimes viewed as more worthless than the pimp. Sweetback is not a pimp and could not do as much as a pimp would, he is much less aggressive. A pimp will work at putting girls on the block, watching them, collecting money, beating them and controlling them. He may also steal and deal in dope and so forth. Sweetback won't do any of this and yet the women love him because he's got such a sweet, sweet back. He will just stay home and the women will bring him everything he needs. He accepts their goods but he doesn't care what they do. So the sweetback is actually more worthless than the pimp, on one level, because he won't take the chances that a pimp would to survive. He has submitted more, almost to the point where he is a vegetable and is just taken care of. So the fact that Sweetback would not stand any more victimization, that he identified with Moo-Moo as being one of the victims, and the fact that Moo-Moo's revolutionary program is pointed to the lowest level of consciousness in the community, means that even though they are unlike characters, even though Moo-Moo is young and Sweetback is older, it is not unlikely that they would be bound together.

When the gamblers get Sweetback and Moo-Moo to the edge of town they tell Sweetback to buy himself a last supper because he is a dead man. Their level of consciousness is so low that they will help him to a point, but they still believe that ultimately the oppressor will triumph and Sweetback will die.

Sweetback and Moo-Moo are determined to survive, however, and they begin their journey. The encounter with the motorcycle gang shows a number of things. First of all it is a triumph of the soul-force (which the women gave Sweetback in the first scene) over all the mechanical developments of the oppressor. When he is challenged to a wrestling duel the gang leader picks up a motorcycle to show brute strength; then with a knife the leader shows how effectively they have mastered this weapon. When the gang leader reveals herself to be a woman, Sweetback knows that she is no match for the weapon he chooses. The gang promises to do him and Moo-Moo in after she does him in, but in the end "the Pres" is laid out on the ground in complete submission. The Black women showed him the way to liberation and he used his knowledge effectively.

Van Peebles is also signifying other things in the motor-cycle gang scene. First of all there is the symbol of the strength of the White woman over the White man (and they don't even know it). Then there is the symbol of the Aryan, the superior race. The president of the gang is big and robust, the image of White superiority. The only criticism I have here is that her hair should have been blond rather than reddish, but the idea gets across. The idea also comes across that the people have the ability to triumph over all these symbols of oppression. Unity will save us.

I should point out that in his duel with the Aryan someone has stuck a derby hat and a silly little tie on Sweetback. It is like a performance, a minstrel show or a cakewalk thing. But Sweetback takes off the derby hat and in that way he tells the others that this is no performance, this is dealing for survival. He deals and he survives, much to their disappointment, and they roar off on their motorcycles, leaving their conquered leader on the ground.

Some of the gang betray Moo-Moo and Sweetback, telling them that since Sweetback has won the duel they will take care of him and Moo-Moo by giving them shelter in a mountain cabin. Instead they send the police. This cabin contains a pool hall, and when the police arrive Moo-Moo and Sweetback are playing pool. When the police enter, Sweetback offers his hands for the cuffs, but then moves to use them to down one policeman. But he is without a weapon to deal with the other one and Moo-Moo is shot. Sweetback uses familiar survival techniques, however, because he deals with what he has available to him. The pool cue becomes a spear, staving the policeman through the chest and drilling him all the way to the hilt of the cue. It is not technology that saves him, it is his ability to use the familiar features of the Black community. This is another important message.

The rest of the scenes show the unity of the community and its creativity in dealing with survival situations. Sweetback sends Moo-Moo on a motorcycle because he is the future. Then he makes it on his feet, by himself. He makes his plea to his feet to do their thing and they never fail him. All he has are his feet and one knife, and he gets by.

In the meantime the police are in the conference room and the commissioner tells them he wants the cop-killers and niggers. Then he calls the Black policemen aside to apologize. They never say a word during the movie, but in their faces you see that they are dead. They are dead because they are separated from the community of victims of which they are a part.

The police vamp on the entire community. They raid a motel and rip out the eyes of one brother. When they realize that he is not Sweetback their reply is "So what?" Melvin Van Peebles is making it plain that we are all Sweetbacks and we are all united in this victimization. At one point they bring Beatle to the morgue to identify a body as Sweetback's; they run their games again with some speech about democracy and communism. They use their idea of bourgeois democracy against the community, but Beatle is a deaf man and has been deaf for a long time. In some respects he is also a blind man because even though he operates a cat house and survives, he cannot read. They are the cause of his problems, for he cannot hear, he cannot see, yet they want him to be a "responsible citizen" and help them. We see that Beatle has been subjected to the Biblical dictum: "Wherefore if thy hand or thy foot offend thee, cut them off and cast them from thee: it is better for thee to enter into life halt or maimed, rather than having two hands or two feet to be cast into everlasting fire. And if thine eye offend thee, pluck it out, and cast it from thee: it is better for thee to enter into life with one eye, rather than having two eyes to be cast into hell fire." (Matthew 18:8-9)

Van Peebles is continuing to signify and send out messages to the Black community. When Beatle sees that the corpse in the morgue is not Sweetback, he breaks up with joy. He gains his hearing in a sense, and also his sight. "For whosoever will save his life shall lose it: and whosoever will lose his life for my sake shall find it." (Matthew 16:25) We see the message very clearly because the camera immediately switches to a shoeshine stand where a brother is shining the man's shoes with his ass and he is really telling the man, for Beatle, what he can do.

So the police go through the community searching for Sweetback, and the people stand as one. They don't know anything. The message here to the community is to "stop snitching," there is need for unity not for revealing our secrets. When I was in the penitentiary I learned the worst crime one inmate can accuse another of is snitching. Van Peebles shows how the community can avoid this and save themselves from their oppressors.

In the meantime we see Sweetback making it through the edges of the city and heading for the desert. He has none of the high-powered technology of the oppressor, but he does have his feet. In one scene we see him going by a large factory; it looks like a chemical plant or something like that. Here you see the drama being symbolized to its fullest, Sweetback with his feet making it on by the man's highest manifestation of technological skill, and you realize that this is the drama developing, the soul-force of the people against the technology of the oppressor. The only question is, which will win? The answer is given by Sweetback in his plea to his feet, he says:

Come on feet
cruise for me
come legs
come on run
come on feet
do your thing
who put the bad mouth on me
anyway the way I pick em up
and put em down
even if it got
my name on it
won't catch me now.

There is Sweetback's answer to the oppressor's technology. Even if the bullet has his name on it, it won't catch him now. Why? Because Sweetback has feet and they will save him.

This is also the beginning of the dialogue between the running Sweetback and the colored angels. As soon as he hits the desert where the situation is really going to be bad, the colored angels come in and try to discourage him. But he has feet, he has heart, and he has courage, and in the dialogue he resists their discouragement as much as he resists the technology of the police, who are always searching.

Now I would like to discuss the movie from a different angle. Instead of a scene-by-scene analysis I want to talk about some of the important ideas signified in various scenes. Some of these ideas have been mentioned already, but I think that it is important to restate them because Melvin Van Peebles uses them so effectively and he is trying to advance our awareness and understanding. So we repeat for added emphasis.

The first key idea or concept which I think the movie presents to us is the need for unity among all the members and institutions within the community and victims. We see the idea of unity between the young and old beautifully expressed in the love and care which the women give to the young boy, and also in the concern Sweetback expresses for Moo-Moo after he realizes that he is truly unified with him. You will recall that Sweetback has an actual dialogue at only six points in the movie; three of these points are in relationship to Moo-Moo. So the revolutionary and the righteous street brother see their functional unity. When Sweetback first downs the cops and saves Moo-Moo, Moo-Moo then asks Sweetback, "Where are we going?" What does Sweetback say? "Where did you get that *we* shit?" This indicates that Sweetback does not understand his need for unity with Moo-Moo. Yet after his encounter with Beatle, Sweetback realizes that he cannot depend on his boss, the guy he should have been able to depend on. But Moo-Moo was somewhere out there being hunted and so was Sweetback—and they were united.

Then when the gamblers are giving Sweetback a ride to the edge of town he spots Moo-Moo and he tells his comrades to stop. This is the second time he speaks about the revolutionary. Now when Moo-Moo gets in the car he tells the brothers who he is, but they still don't see their need for unity because to them he is not Moo-Moo, he is the guy who got their partner into trouble. They blame the victim rather than those who victimize him, but this is because of their low level of awareness. Sweetback did the same earlier, but he was revolutionized by his awareness of the true situation. Our unity will come out of consciousness, and this is the point to raise the consciousness of the Black community.

The film also demonstrates the functional unity between the present and the future. Once again we see this in the women giving nourishment and love to the boy who is their future, their liberator. If they did not feed him now and give him the strength to survive until his revolutionary consciousness is aroused, then he would not be able to liberate them. So pending the revolution they must do all they can to help him survive.

We also see the unity between the present and the future

when Sweetback visits the church. He receives no help but gets a little more understanding of the true nature of his contribution to the community. The minister tells him that what he did for Moo-Moo was the correct thing. He says, "You saved the plant that they were planning to nip in the bud. That's why the Man's down on you." Then later when Sweetback has another chance to escape, but without Moo-Moo, he tells the Black motorcyclist to take the young brother instead. The motorcyclist asks Sweetback if he knows what he is doing, and he replies, "He's our future, Brer. Take him."

The film also demonstrates the value of unity among the entire Black community. This is shown at the very beginning when the movie titles appear indicating that the movie is starring THE BLACK COMMUNITY. There is no hero, there is no one outstanding individual, there is the community. At the end there are some names of participants, but it does not even tell what roles they played. This is all an attempt to play down the individualistic approach to our survival in favor of an expression of unity among the entire community.

This unity is also demonstrated by the fact that Sweetback has almost no dialogue in the entire movie. He says hardly anything at all. Why? Because the movie is not starring Sweetback, it is starring the Black community. Most of the audiences at the movie are Black and they talk to the screen. They supply the dialogue because all of us are Sweetback; we are all in the same predicament of being victims. This is clearly seen when Sweetback comes back to Beatle for help. Sweetback says nothing, but Beatle lets it come out of both ends. The audience replies to Beatle for Sweetback, and they supply the dialogue. This happens throughout the film. So the thing to do is not just see the film, but also to recognize how you the viewer are also an actor in the film, for you are as much a victim of this oppressive system as Sweetback.

The unity of the community is shown throughout the film

and we should get the message the brother is signifying to us. When the community sets the police car afire and saves Sweetback, that is an expression of unity. When they deny ever having seen him in order to permit him to escape, that is an expression of unity. When the police raid the motel and rip the brother's eye out, they say, "So what?" when told this is not Sweetback. But it *is* Sweetback, in a sense, because the brother is another victim like all of us. When Beatle is rolled up to the morgue and realizes that the body they show him is not Sweetback, he sees his unity as a victim with his brother who he failed to help, who is also a victim. And Beatle cracks up laughing; they are unified. And in the next scene at the shoeshine stand Van Peebles signifies to the man that he can kiss his ass.

Another expression of unity in the film is the power symbol. When the minister tells Sweetback the significance of the job he has done for Moo-Moo, he then says a Black Ave Maria for him and ends up giving him the power sign—unity. Then when Moo-Moo gets on the motorcycle to escape, leaving Sweetback behind, this is different from their first parting. They give each other a soul shake. So that even though they go separate ways they are unified.

Finally the film demonstrates the importance of unity and love between Black men and women. This is shown again in the scene where the woman makes love to the young boy, which in fact baptizes him into his true manhood. Also, when the woman makes love to Sweetback and then gets the handcuffs off him, we see that these are not sex scenes, they are love scenes in a very holy and righteous context. The second woman wants Sweetback to beg, but he has been transformed. His baptism in the blood transformed him: he has ripped off his oppressors and he is truly a man. He can never beg again, and he does not.

For a long time the Black community has been a collection of people who survive together in one place, but unity is essential for liberation as well as survival. When we have this unity the faith of one becomes the faith of another, as in the case of Sweetback and Moo-Moo. When we have our consciousness increased, victimizers will always try to prevent this unity. And we must understand that the victimizers will always try to prevent this unity.

Another idea the film gets across is the different point of view between the victim and the victimizer. The victimizers cannot accept the reality and truth of the view of the victims, and therefore they say that the victims are always wrong in their view of reality. Indeed, they even go so far as to signify that the victims cannot control and direct their own lives. This is seen first of all in the fact that the film is labeled with an "X" rating. The oppressors see Sweetback as a sex film, but if we truly understand ourselves and unify with Sweetback, we will see that the film advocates a bloody overthrow of the oppressor. Melvin Van Peebles is righteously signifying.

The view of the victims is seen in many ways. One of them is in the understanding of Moo-Moo and Sweetback. They both know that they are victims, although Moo-Moo has not really gotten his complete program together for the community. Yet they seek the same goals of freedom and liberation, and they recognize that sometimes you have to use stern stuff to accomplish your goals. They also recognize that even though the community may not support you entirely, they will support you to a point. Therefore, you must go as far as the community will go, and then move out on your own, leading the people to a higher level of consciousness. Sweetback relies on the community much more than Moo-Moo because he understands that revolution is a process, going from A to B to C and so forth, rather than trying to get the people to jump from A to Z.

The oppressor does not understand this, he does not understand the strength of the will of the people. When the two policemen catch Sweetback after he leaves Beatle's place, they are friendly because they cannot accept the idea that the community will free itself. So they ask Sweetback how many people were in the ambush? How did they work it? The oppressors cannot accept the idea that the oppressed could do this without a lot of planning, without a large number of people. It was only Sweetback and Moo-Moo, but to the victimizer it had to be more than that. A difference in point of view, a point of view which is too often used to control us, but we must make our own point of view prevail.

Another difference in point of view is seen with the chains which are used on Sweetback twice in the film. To the oppressor they are the chains which keep us in a submissive position, but each time for Sweetback, the oppressed, they become tools of liberation. We will be even stronger when we learn how to turn the oppressor's tools against him rather than submitting to them.

Another idea which Melvin Van Peebles puts across is the uselessness of cultist behavior in our struggle for survival and liberation. In earlier issues of the paper I have talked about the revolutionary cultist, the cultural cultist, and the religious cultist. Van Peebles strikes some heavy blows at the religious and cultural cultists. For example, the minister understands that he is not moving the people toward their true liberation. He tells Sweetback that what he is doing is giving the people a hype that gives them a little happiness, but he then goes on to say that Moo-Moo and the younger guys are laying down the real religion. So this is a blow against those religions in the Black community which do not help people deal with the conditions which drive them to their knees, but instead want to keep the people on their knees.

The strongest blow against cultist behavior, however, is saved for the cultural cultists. We see this in the African garb which the minister is wearing. This is signifying that a lot of cultural nationalism and the meaningless religions in the community are deceiving the people in the same ways.

In another way the film makes this point more strongly and also indicates the true way to liberation. When Sweetback arrives at the gambler's den, the men around the table are engaged in a conversation. The manager has complained to Sweetback that he cannot even make any money on this operation because he is paying off so many others. The cultural cultist offers many empty solutions to our oppression and this scene hits at these solutions.

After the manager's speech one gambler says, "And Africa shall stretch forth her arms," and then another replies, "Yeah, and bring back a bloody stump." Now we have to understand the true issue in order to see this as a blow to cultural nationalists, who are cultural cultists (with African clothes, bones and other things, but no ways to liberate the people). Cultural cultists, who try to claim that they have the way, often use this scripture to support their ideas: "Princes shall come out of Egypt; Ethiopia shall soon stretch out her hands unto God." (Psalms 68:31) You can see that what Van Peebles is signifying is that those who use such meaningless arguments to mislead the people have nothing to offer, because when they stretch forth their arms, they will draw back a bloody stump. Still, however, Van Peebles does show us how a bloody stump may not be a meaningless thing if we get out of that cultist bag. How does he do this? He shows the blood on Sweetback's arms each time he downs the cops. In his first baptism by blood there is blood all the way up to his elbow. And later when he downs the cops in the poolroom, there is blood up to his elbow again. That is the true route to liberation: stern action when the situation demands that you seize the time and turn away from cultist behavior.

There is another key idea which comes through repeatedly. That is the ability of the people to survive even under the hardest conditions. We do this by using the means available to us and never worrying about the fact that we don't have all the technology that the oppressor has. You will recall that Sweetback was in chains and in the back of the police car when the people "washed" it with gasoline. What did the brother do? He made it out of the car and then walked right through the police and firemen who were arriving to try and deal with the situation. He walked right through them—he did not panic and run, he just calmly turned a situation of oppression to his advantage.

Later on when Sweetback and Moo-Moo had separated for the final time, the brother was faced with a very difficult situation, and he had very little to carry him through. But when the colored angels began to get down on him he told them, "I got feet." This was again symbolizing survival. It was not simply that he had feet, however, he also had the ability to use the technology of the oppressor in his own interest. He did not become discouraged because he had no car. Van Peebles could have had him steal a car, but instead he had Sweetback use the basic skills of survival with nothing but the things he had learned for surviving the oppressor for so many years on the block. He doesn't have a car, but he rides: on the top of a truck, inside the back of another truck, on a freight train. He uses the oppressor's technology, but in his own interest.

He also survives by using the system against itself. He meets another traveler and pays him to change clothes and run when he is chased. This throws the police off his trail and helps him survive, but it also means that he ends up with clothes which are much more suitable for his long run across the desert. Later in the film when he is near the border and the dogs are after him, the two men (the owner of the dogs and the policeman) get into a fight between themselves about whether the dogs should be untied. This is all to Sweetback's advantage, turning the oppressors against each other, and he makes his escape.

In another way he survives the way that the Black community has always survived—by using the resources at his command even though they are not the resources others would use. Survival forces some very harsh decisions on us.

When his wound is causing him to suffer, he urinates upon the earth and uses his own urine to make a mudpack, which he applies to the wound. It produces a rapid healing. These are the kind of home remedies we have long had to use because we could not get proper medical attention. Later, we see him bathing his face in a pool of muddy water. It sustains him. When I saw it, I thought of that song which says "I'd rather drink muddy water, and sleep in a hollow log than stay here and be treated like a dirty dog."

These are survival techniques all the audience can identify with because they realize they are necessary. They don't identify with the time he catches that lizard and downs it, raw. But this is no different from the times when we had to eat the chitterlings, hog maws, and other foods, not because we wanted to, but because that was all we had to eat. We may deny it, we may not identify with it, but it carried us through. And the point we should understand is that if you do not submit to the oppressor you may be forced to make some harsh decisions, eat some undesirable foods, but this is better than being well-fed in some social prison.

Sweetback has only one tool with him, his knife, and he uses it very effectively. It reminds me of that point in *The Wretched of the Earth* where Fanon says that if you don't have a gun then a knife will do. He uses his knife to escape at the rock concert by pretending to make love to the girl in the bushes. He uses the knife against the lizard. And then when he hears the dogs coming after him, he again pulls it out and uses it, and he really deals. But we should know it would be this way because earlier in the poolroom when he was facing the policeman with a gun, what did Sweetback have? A tool the community knows how to use very effectively, a pool cue. But he did not use it to down pool balls, he turned it into a spear and downed the oppressor. You don't need a gun. What you need is the consciousness of what it will take to survive and prevail in any given situation, and then act accordingly.

What I have done is to give you a scene-by-scene analysis

of the film, then an analysis of some of the major ideas and concepts. Now I will show how the movie also raises the consciousness of the community by analyzing it in terms of some aspects of the ideology of the Black Panther Party.

We see ideology as a systematic way of thinking about phenomena, not as some set of abstract conclusions. Our approach is one that uses dialectical materialism, which holds that contradictions are the ruling principle of the universe. Everywhere, in all of life—the social forces, the natural forces, and the biological and physical forces—we can find contradictions. What we mean is that in every phenomenon there is a contradiction between opposing forces which struggle to gain domination over each other. We call this the thesis and anti-thesis, or the unity of the opposites. Because these opposites are both unified and constantly in struggle with one another, they give motion to the matter composing the phenomenon. So we say that matter is constantly in motion, or constantly in a state of transformation. The transformation takes place in a dialectical manner, with the thesis struggling against the antithesis. These are the contradictions. The struggle is resolved in a synthesis that contains elements of the old contradictions, but at a higher level. Then a new set of contradictions will arise.

The essence of the ideology of the Black Panther Party is that we recognize that matter is constantly in transformation in a dialectical manner. But when we understand this and understand the forces in operation, we can control them and direct them in a manner which is beneficial for the community. Therefore what we want to do is understand the contradictions within every aspect of the Black community and move on them by trying to increase the positive side of each contradiction until it comes to dominate the negative side. This is how we define power: the ability to define phenomena and make it act in a desired manner.

If you understand where the Panther is coming from, you will understand that Sweet Sweetback is a beautiful exemplification of Black Power, for what he does is decide how he wants things to come out and then he makes them act in a desired manner. The movie is also an exemplification of the dialectical analysis and the constant transformation of phenomena. I don't know whether Melvin Van Peebles was aware of this when he made the movie, but it does have these features. It gives us lots of insight and understanding.

For example, we say that all phenomena contain contradictions with positive and negative qualities. To control the situation, then, what you must do is increase the positive qualities of any phenomena until they dominate the negative qualities. Sweetback does this on a number of occasions. Take for example the chains. The handcuffs are definitely negative when they are used to keep him in submission, but when Sweetback realizes that he can ignore the beating of Moo-Moo no longer, what is he to use for a weapon? Thus the same chains which were used to bind become tools of liberation. Their positive qualities are used to overcome their negative qualities. He did this again when he was caught by the police in the poolroom. He offered his hands for the chains. Not because he wanted them, but because he realized that this would put the police off their guard, and also give him another weapon to use against them. We see this again when the police are using helicopters, cars, guns and the radio to track down Sweetback. What does he use? Their technology, but in a positive way. He hitches rides on trucks and trains, and they help to deliver him from the jaws of the monsters, who are using the most advanced technology to try and capture him. If we understand dialectical materialism we will understand more about how to look at both the positive and negative qualities of phenomena so that we can control our destiny.

The film also shows the positive and negative features of community institutions. In other articles I have said that the

Black Panther Party was wrong in its blanket condemnations of community institutions, instead of analyzing their qualities. The film shows the positive and negative features of the church, for example. The minister is saying to Sweetback that he has nothing to offer the community, he can only give the people a hype which will bring them a little bit of happiness in their misery. Also he cannot offer Sweetback a hideout because the police ("the Man") knows everything. This shows his negative and reactionary side. At the same time we see his positive and progressive side because he is operating a withdrawal center where people addicted to drugs can come and dry out. There is no blanket condemnation. He shows the church making a real contribution to the survival of the community. What needs to happen is for people with a higher level of consciousness to increase the positive contribution the church makes until the positive becomes the most important feature of the church. Then it will be able to do more for the people.

The same is true in the case of the gambler. He cannot offer Sweetback any money; he is exploiting and he is also exploited. So when the brother really needs help he has no money to give him. What's more, the advice he gives is worthless because he says that Sweetback is dead and tells him to get himself a last supper. But there is also a positive quality to the gambler since he gives Sweetback and Moo-Moo a ride for part of the way. Actually, he can give them a ride all the way to the border, but he will only give them a ride to the edge of town where they run into the motorcycle gang. But the point is made very well: that you have to work with the people as far as they will go and not jump too far ahead by forcing them to do things they do not want to do at that particular level of consciousness. So he carries the positive qualities of the gambler as far as they will go and then strikes out again. This is taking your revolution from point A to point B rather than from A to Z in one step. We have to find out what the people will do and get them to do that much.

The progression of the people as their consciousness increases is shown in the case of Beatle. At first, Beatle is an individual surviving at a basic level, running a cat house and then giving up one of his men in order to continue to operate. Then Beatle offers advice which is nothing more than a pile of dung. Next we see Beatle going through the revolutionizing process. If he knew where Sweetback was he would have told on him, but because he was "deaf" before and because he cannot cooperate with the police, they actually deafen him—the conditions revolutionize him. When we next see Beatle it is in the morgue scene and he cracks up as he realizes that Sweetback has escaped. They are unified. Beatle has seen that he also is a victim and there can be no cooperation with the oppressor because they will bleed you to death; if you want to live you have to resist. And the shoeshine man uses his ass on the shoes of his oppressor.

There is also a progression within the community. They rescue Sweetback and aid him as much as they can in his escape, then they become deaf to their oppressors. That is a way of hearing the plea of Sweetback to his feet and giving him enough lead time to let his feet do their job.

The community's progression is also shown in the transformation of the colored angels. We hear the voices of the community as the police search for Sweetback, but when he reaches the desert we hear the voices of the angels in a dialogue with Sweetback. On the record Melvin Van Peebles refers to this as an opera (an opera is merely a story told in song) and the dialogue between Sweetback and the angels is really Sweet Sweetback's Baadasssss Song. In the book Van Peebles refers to the angels as colored angels, then he refers to them as Black angels. On the record he refers to them as Reggin (spell it backwards) angels. The point is that the angels are against the interests of Sweetback, but they are transformed because their interests are in fact the same as his. This is the dialogue with the angels, the Baadasssss Song:

If you can't beat 'em join 'em
That's what they say

You talking 'bout yesterday

You can't go on like that Sweetback
Not long as your face is Black

Yeah, I'm Black and I'm keepin' on
Keepin' on the same ole way

They bopped your mama
They bopped your papa

Won't bop me

They bopped your sister
They bopped your brother

They won't bop me

THEY BURNED OUR MAMAS
THEY BEAT OUR PAPAS
THEY TRICKED OUR SISTERS
THEY CHAINED OUR BROTHERS
WON'T BLEED ME
WON'T BLEED ME
WON'T BLEED ME

They bled your mama
They bled your papa
But he won't bleed me

Use your Black ass from sun to sun
Niggers scared and pretend they don't see
Deep down dirty dog scared

Just like you Sweetback

Just like I used to be
Work your Black behind to the gums
And you supposed to thomas tell he done

You got to thomas Sweetback
They bled your brother
They bled your sister
Yeah, but they won't bleed me

Progress Sweetback

That's what he wants you to believe

No progress Sweetback

He ain't stopped clubbing us for 400 years
And he don't intend to for a million

He sure treat us bad Sweetback
We can make him do us better

Chicken ain't nothing but a bird
White man ain't nothing but a turd
Nigger ain't shit

Get my hands on a trigger

You talkin' revolution Sweetback

I wanta get off these knees

You talkin' revolution Sweetback

You can't make it on wings
Wheels or steel Sweetback
We got feet
You can't get away on wings
wheels or steel Sweetback
Niggers got feet

He bled your brother
He bled your sister
Your brother and your sister too
How come it took me so long to see
How he get us to use each other
Niggers scared

We got to get it together if he kicks a brother
It gotta be like he kickin' your mother

They hype you into sopping the
Marrow out your own bones
Justice is blind
Yeah and white too

Justice is blind
The way she acts she gotta be
The man is jive
Not too jive to have his game
Uptight in your kinky bean

Stand tall Sweetback he
Ain't gonna let you
I'm standing tall anyway

The man know everything Sweetback
The man know everything
Then he ought to know I'm
Tired of him fuckin' with me

Use your feet baby
Run motherfucka
Run Sweetback
He wont bleed me

We can see the transformation of the angels if we see the opera in relationship to the scenes in the film. When he arrives at the desert, the most difficult and lonesome part of his whole trip, the colored angels chastise and ridicule him. They believe, like the gambler, that he is a dead man and it will only be a matter of time until he is caught. So they signify about how the "Man" bopped his brother and sister, how he bled his mama and poppa, and how he will get Sweetback. But Sweetback is determined because he knows they won't bop him, they won't bleed him. Why? "I got feet." All he is signifying is that I can deal, and I can survive.

When he uses his urine mixed with mud to make the pack which heals his wounds, the angels begin to change. They see, too, that he will survive, so they start to become Black. They recognize that they too are like Sweetback and they point out that they have been also treated badly, but they have been acting like Uncle Toms. Sweetback is going to get his finger on a trigger, get off his knees, and fight a revolution. So when he makes the mudpack, the Black angels tell him to run, they want him to deal, now, they don't want him to Tom. They too have been transformed because Sweetback has increased their positive qualities by showing them it is not necessary to submit all the time. At some point you have got to get off your knees.

Their transformation continues because when the police looses the hound dogs (slave dogs) after Sweetback and he draws his knife, the Black angels begin to sing "This little light of mine, I'm going to let it shine." This is the first time we have heard this song since Sweetback's baptism into his manhood. The growth he experienced the first time this song was sung, the way he learned from those women in the house of prostitution is going to serve him again. They gave him love and strength because he was their future, their liberator, and their training is going to serve him, now that he is older. The angels are transformed and Sweetback survives. This brings us to the end of the movie and the negation of the negation. At the beginning, the community of the oppressed was in contradiction with the oppressors. The oppressed were trying to survive, but the oppressors would not permit that, they wanted more. They wanted to bleed them to death and completely dominate them. They wanted to dominate by dividing the community: Sweetback against Moo-Moo, Beatle against Sweetback. This continued oppression led the people to realize that their salvation would only come through unity, and unity would only come through heightened levels of consciousness. So they unify and Sweetback revolts against the oppressors and makes good his escape. Many do not believe he will make it; their consciousness is not as high as his. He is reaching for the stars—making it to the border—but they will only take him to the edge of town.

Sweetback has his high level of consciousness, that is to say, he is a Sweet Sweetback because he has come to understand that freedom, liberation, and the ability to love requires that first of all you have to recapture the holy grail; you have to restore your dignity and manhood by destroying the one who took it from you. When you do that, even if you do not completely escape, you are a dangerous man because after that the oppressor knows that you will no longer be submissive. Therefore, ripping off your oppressor is the first step toward freedom and love.

This understanding did not come easily to Sweetback. He attempted to look away from Moo-Moo, and then, after rescuing him, he attempted to make it on his own, only to be misled by Beatle. This put him in the situation of a revolutionary in the sense that he knew then that he could not find a place of refuge within the system without a whole transformation of the conditions of oppression.

I say this because many people think that revolutionaries are made out of some kind of abstract predicaments. This is not so. They are transformed by a particular set of situations that are sometimes unique to each individual. What brings one person into his revolutionary consciousness is different from what will bring another, but when we reach that point we realize that we are all unified as victims. That is what happened to Sweetback, Moo-Moo, Beatle, the angels, and the community in the film. That is why the film stars the Black community—all of us. We must understand our unity and also how we must heighten our consciousness.

So like I said, we have the negation of the negation. The

oppressor who wanted to exploit Sweetback and Beatle ends up beaten by them because they will take his stuff no longer. The contradiction between the community as represented by Sweetback, and the oppressor as represented by the dogs, has been resolved.

However, each synthesis leads to new contradictions. Right until the end Melvin Van Peebles is signifying and conveying a message to us. What is the new contradiction? Sweetback has killed two dogs, but one is still there, refreshing himself in the water mingled with the blood of the other dogs. If Sweetback got two dogs, who is going to get the other? That is the dog we must down. So the film ends with the words "Watch Out." This has a dual meaning. It is telling all the many Sweetbacks across the land to watch out for that third dog and be prepared to deal when he shows up. It also says to the oppressor to watch out for the Sweetbacks across the land because they are coming to collect some dues. Righteously signifying.

When Bobby and I started the Black Panther Party, we wanted to build in the Black community the love, the sacredness, and the unity we need so desperately. This is still our goal and we try to help the community survive by administering our many survival programs. Sweet Sweetback helps to put forth the ideas of what we must do to build that community. We need to see it often and learn from it.

On the Peace Movement:
August 15, 1969

The Peace Movement is extremely important, more important than I thought it was two years ago. The reason I place so much emphasis upon the Peace Movement now is because I see that if peace were to come about it would revolutionize the basic economic composition of the country.

Let me explain. We all know now that this is a garrison state, a warfare state. And not by accident. When capitalism can no longer expand, it looks for other avenues, other deposits, other places to increase its interests. At this moment, the super capitalists (General Motors, Chrysler, General Dynamics, and all of the super companies—I understand about seventy-six people control the whole economy of this country) and their companies are the main contractors for the Pentagon. In other words these companies are putting their overexpanded capitalistic surplus into military equipment. This military equipment is then placed in foreign countries such as Vietnam or the Dominican Republic which are the final depositories for expendable goods. With the wedding of industry and the Pentagon, there is a new avenue to invest in. Military equipment is an expendable avenue, because the purpose of the equipment is to explode therefore you have to keep building new ones. A perpetual process.

We know that the U.S. has a secret pact with Thailand. These pacts are all part of a super-plan to keep the economy going. What would happen then, if peace were to come about? There would not be that final depository for expendable goods; the surplus would then be turned back into the country. The military plants, the related defense plants, and industrial plants would be brought to a grinding halt.

This is why you have some of the union representatives supporting the war effort. This is why the AFL-CIO supported the invasion of the Dominican Republic. It forced out Juan Bosch for the simple reason that they know that as long as the war goes on, they can exploit the people through taxation and human lives. We sent soldiers, you see, brothers, because they are expendable too; people are expendable.

One of the favored arguments of the capitalists is that America is not an imperialistic country because the traditional method of the imperialist is to go into a developing country, rape if of its raw materials, refine them either in the colony or the mother country, or refine them and sell them back at a high price to the colonized people. And the argument is that "America is not doing that. We don't need any equipment or raw materials out of Vietnam." And this is very true. This contradiction sort of puzzled me for a while and I couldn't really answer it so I just talked around it. But now I understand that something new has happened; that with the wedding of science and industry, the industrial plants in America have solved the basic problem of raw materials through synthetics and the knowledge of using raw materials that are already here in a variety of ways, therefore keeping the plants going. The favored argument of the capitalist is "We must be there to stop communism or wars of subversion." What is overlooked is the fact that the super-capitalists know we don't need to rape the country. I think Cuba was the turning point away from the traditional colonized country.

Another argument is that they need the strategic military positions. But we know that the U.S. does not need any strategic military positions because they already have enough equipment to defend this country from any point in the world if attacked. So they could only be there to use this developing country as a depository for expendable goods.

In traditional imperialism, people from the mother country usually go to the colony, set up the government, and the leaders of the military, but this is not so in America. People from the mother country have not gone to the colonized country of Vietnam and jockeyed for position, but the profit has all been turned back into America. The defense contractors now jockey for position in the mother country for the defense contracts. Then they set up a puppet government or a military regime so that they can supply these developing countries with military equipment. They really do not want to be in Vietnam or any of the developing countries because they feel (and they have done this) that they have bought off the militaries in these various developing countries so that they will only be an arm of the Pentagon. The military regime in Greece is a good example. They have full control of the military officers, paying them high salaries so they will not have to send American troops and disturb the mother country.

But what happens when one battalion of military is defeated? Then you send in reinforcements for the defeated puppet army in that developing country. The whole government becomes subject to the army. And the army becomes suspicious of the civil government in these developing countries because they are told by the Pentagon through indoctrination and money that the civil government is a communist threat to the nation. Military coups follow, and this is what happens over and over in countries supported by the U.S.

We have actually an imperialistic variation of imperialism. The jockeying for positions of power is inside of the mother country now, so, in fact, the American people have become colonized.

At one time I thought that only Blacks were colonized. But I think we have to change our rhetoric to an extent because the whole American people have been colonized, if you view exploitation as a colonized effect. Seventy-six companies have exploited everyone. American people are a colonized people even more so than the people in developing countries where the military operates.

This is why the Peace Movement is so important. If the Peace Movement is successful, then the revolution will be successful. If the Peace Movement fails, then the revolution in the mother country fails. In other words, the people would be pushed so uptight once war were to stop that the whole economy would go down the drain. Only a planned economy could combat the chaos that the absence of incentive would cause. Now war is the incentive for the military contractors.

This is why it is very important that we have communications with the Peace Movement. Not only should we communicate with it, we should actually get out and support it fully in various ways including literature and demonstrations.

We have to realize our position and we have to know ourselves and know our enemies. A thousand wars and a thousand victories. And until we know who the enemy is and what the situation is we will only be marking time. Even the Peace Movement doesn't compromise our defense principles. We still defend ourselves against attack and against aggression. But overall, we are advocating the end to all wars. But, yet, we support the self-defense of the Vietnamese people and all the people who are struggling.

The Women's Liberation and Gay Liberation Movements:
August 15, 1970

During the past few years strong movements have developed among women and among homosexuals seeking their liberation. There has been some uncertainty about how to relate to these movements.

Whatever your personal opinions and your insecurities about homosexuality and the various liberation movements among homosexuals and women (and I speak of the homosexuals and women as oppressed groups), we should try to unite with them in a revolutionary fashion. I say "whatever your insecurities are" because as we very well know, sometimes our first instinct is to want to hit a homosexual in the mouth, and want a woman to be quiet. We want to hit a homosexual in the mouth because we are afraid we might be homosexual; and we want to hit the woman or shut her up because we are afraid that she might castrate us, or take the nuts that we might not have to start with.

We must gain security in ourselves and therefore have respect and feelings for all oppressed people. We must not use the racist attitude that the White racists use against our people because they are Black and poor. Many times the poorest White person is the most racist because he is afraid that he might lose something, or discover something that he does not have. So you're some kind of threat to him. This kind of psychology is in operation when we view oppressed people and we are angry with them because of their particular kind of behavior, or their particular kind of deviation from the established norm.

Remember, we have not established a revolutionary value system; we are only in the process of establishing it. I do not remember our ever constituting any value that said that a revolutionary must say offensive things towards homosexuals, or that a revolutionary should make sure that women do not speak out about their own particular kind of oppression. As a matter of fact, it is just the opposite: we say that we recognize the women's right to be free. We have not said much about the homosexual at all, but we must relate to the homosexual movement because it is a real thing. And I know through reading, and through my life experience and observations that homosexuals are not given freedom and liberty by anyone in the society. They might be the most oppressed people in the society.

And what made them homosexual? Perhaps it's a phenomenon that I don't understand entirely. Some people say that it is the decadence of capitalism. I don't know if that is the case; I rather doubt it. But whatever the case is, we know that homosexuality is a fact that exists, and we must understand it in its purest form: that is, a person should have the freedom to use his body in whatever way he wants.

That is not endorsing things in homosexuality that we wouldn't view as revolutionary. But there is nothing to say that a homosexual cannot also be a revolutionary. And maybe I'm now injecting some of my prejudice by saying that "even a homosexual can be a revolutionary." Quite the contrary, maybe a homosexual could be the most revolutionary.

When we have revolutionary conferences, rallies, and demonstrations, there should be full participation of the gay liberation movement and the women's liberation movement. Some groups might be more revolutionary than others. We should not use the actions of a few to say that they are all reactionary or counterrevolutionary, because they are not.

We should deal with the factions just as we deal with any other group or party that claims to be revolutionary. We should try to judge, somehow, whether they are operating in a sincere revolutionary fashion and from a really oppressed situation. (And we will grant that if they are women they are probably oppressed.) If they do things that are unrevolutionary or counterrevolutionary, then criticize that action. If we feel that the group in spirit means to be revolutionary in practice, but they make mistakes in interpretation of the revolutionary philosophy, or they do not understand the dialectics of the social forces in operation, we should criticize that and not criticize them because they are women trying to be free. And the same is true for homosexuals. We should never say a whole movement is dishonest when in fact they are trying to be honest. They are just making honest mistakes. Friends are allowed to make mistakes. The enemy is not allowed to make mistakes because his whole existence is a mistake, and we suffer from it. But the women's liberation front and gay liberation front are our friends, they are potential allies, and *we need as many allies as possible.*

We should be willing to discuss the insecurities that many people have about homosexuality. When I say "insecurities," I mean the fear that they are some kind of threat to our manhood. I can understand this fear. Because of the long conditioning process which builds insecurity in the American male, homosexuality might produce certain hangups in us. I have hang-ups myself about male homosexuality. But on the other hand, I have no hang-up about female homosexuality. And that is a phenomenon in itself. I think it is probably because male homosexuality is a threat to me and female homosexuality is not.

We should be careful about using those terms that might turn our friends off. The terms "faggot" and "punk" should be deleted from our vocabulary, and especially we should not attach names normally designed for homosexuals to men who are enemies of the people, such as Nixon or Mitchell. Homosexuals are not enemies of the people.

We should try to form a working coalition with the gay liberation and women's liberation groups. We must always handle social forces in the most appropriate manner.

To the Revolutionary People's Constitutional Convention: September 5, 1970*

Two centuries ago the United States was a new nation conceived in liberty and dedicated to life, liberty, and the pursuit of happiness. The conditions which prevailed in the nation and the assumptions upon which its foundations were built ensured that the United States would come to its maturity under circumstances which required that the life of a substantial proportion of its citizens be nothing more than a prison of poverty, and happiness nothing more than laughing to keep from crying.

The United States of America was born at a time when the nation covered relatively little land, a narrow strip of political divisions on the Eastern seaboard. The United States of America was born at a time when the population was small and fairly homogeneous both racially and culturally. Thus the people called Americans were a different people in a different place. Furthermore, they had a different economic system. The small population and the fertile land available meant that with the agricultural emphasis on the economy, people were able to advance according to their motivation and ability. It was an agricultural economy and with the circumstances surrounding it Democratic Capitalism flourished in the new nation.

The following years were to see this new nation rapidly develop into a multi-limbed giant. The new nation acquired land and spread from a narrow strip on the Eastern sea-

* An address delivered to the Plenary Session in Philadelphia, Pa.

board to cover almost the entire continent. The new nation acquired a population to fill this newly acquired land. This population was drawn from the continents of Africa, Asia, Europe and South America. Thus a nation conceived by homogeneous people of a small number and in a small area grew into a nation of a heterogeneous people, comprising a large number and spread across an entire continent. This change in the fundamental characteristics of the nation and its people substantially changed the nature of American society. Furthermore, the social changes were marked by economic changes. A rural and agricultural economy became an urban and industrialized economy, as farming was replaced by manufacturing. The Democratic Capitalism of our early days became caught up in a relentless drive to obtain profits until the selfish motivation for profit eclipsed the unselfish principles of democracy. Thus 200 years later we have an overdeveloped economy which is so infused with the need for profit that we have replaced *Democratic Capitalism with Bureaucratic Capitalism*. The free opportunity of all men to pursue their economic ends has been replaced by constraints (confinement) placed upon Americans by the large corporations which control and direct our economy. They have sought to increase their profits at the expense of the people, and particularly at the expense of the racial and ethnic minorities.

The history of the United States, as distinguished from the promise of the idea of the United States, leads us to the conclusion that our sufferance is basic to the functioning of the government of the United States. We see this when we note the basic contradictions found in the history of this nation. The government, the social conditions, and the legal documents which brought freedom from oppression, which brought human dignity and human rights to one portion of the people of this nation, had entirely opposite consequences for another portion of the people. While the majority group achieved their basic human rights, the minorities achieved alienation from the lands of their fathers and slavery. The evidence for this is clear and incontrovertible.

We find evidence for *majority freedom and minority oppression* in the fact that the expansion of the United States Government and the acquisition of lands was at the unjust expense of the American Indians, who are the original possessors of the land and still its legitimate heirs. The long march of the Cherokees on the "Trail of Tears" and the actual disappearance of many other Indian nations testify to the unwillingness and inability of this government and this government's Constitution to incorporate racial minorities.

We find evidence for majority freedom and minority oppression in the fact that even while the early settlers were proclaiming their freedom, they were deliberately and systematically depriving Africans of their freedom. These basic contradictions were further exacerbated (made angry) by acts which implicitly admitted that the majority was wrong but unwilling to do right. Thus when the Declaration of Independence was drafted, the Founding Fathers considered the slave as equivalent to three-fifths of a man. Thus when the slaves were emancipated the descendants of the Founding Fathers compromised that freedom to gain further territory. These compromises were so basic to the thinking of our forebears that legal attempts to correct the contradictions through Constitutional amendments and civil-rights laws have produced no change in our condition. We are still a people without equal protection and due process of law. We recognize then that the oppressive acts of the United States Government when contrasted with the testaments of freedom, carry forward a basic contradiction found in all the legal documents upon which this government is based.

Generation after generation of the majority group have been born, they have worked, and they have seen the fruits of their labors in the life, liberty and happiness of their children and grandchildren. Generation after generation of Black people in America have been born, they have worked, and they have seen the fruits of their labors in the life, liberty, and happiness of the children and grandchildren of their oppressors, while their own descendants wallow in the mire of poverty and deprivation, holding only to the hope of change in the future. This hope has sustained us for many years and has led us to suffer the administrations of a corrupt government. At the dawn of the twentieth century this hope led us to formulate a civil-rights movement in the belief that this government would eventually fulfill its promise to Black people. We did not recognize, however, that any attempt to complete the promise of an eighteenth-century revolution in the framework of a twentieth-century government was doomed to failure. The descendants of that small company of original settlers of this land are not among the common people of today, they have become a small ruling class in control of a world-wide economic system. The Constitution set up by their ancestors to serve the people no longer does so, for the people have changed. The people of the eighteenth century have become the ruling class of the twentieth century, and the people of the twentieth century are the descendants of the slaves and dispossessed of the eighteenth century. The Constitution set up to serve the people of the eighteenth century now serves the ruling class of the twentieth century, and the people of today stand waiting for a foundation of their own life, liberty and pursuit of happiness. The Civil-Rights Movement has not produced this foundation, and it cannot produce this foundation because of the nature of the United States society and economy. The vision of the Civil-Rights Movement is to achieve goals which have been altered by 200 years of change. Thus the Civil-Rights Movement and similar movements have produced no foundation for life, liberty, and the pursuit of happiness. They have produced humiliating programs of welfare and unemployment compensation, programs with sufficient form to deceive the people but with insufficient substance to change the fundamental distribution of power and resources in this country.

Moreover, while these movements attempt to get minorities into the system, we note that the government continues its pattern of practices which contradict its democratic rhetoric. We recognize now that we see history repeating itself, but on an international as well as national scale. The relentless drive for profit led this nation to colonize, oppress, and exploit its minorities. This profit drive took this nation from democratic capitalism and underdevelopment to bureaucratic capitalism and overdevelopment. Now we see that this small ruling class continues its profit drive by oppressing and exploiting the peoples of the world. Throughout the world the lumpenproletariat is crushed so that the profits of American industry can continue to flow. Throughout the world the freedom struggles of oppressed people are opposed by this government because they are a threat to bureaucratic capitalism in the United States of America.

We gather here to let it be known at home and abroad that a nation conceived in liberty and dedicated to life, liberty, and the pursuit of happiness has in its maturity become an imperialist power dedicated to death, oppression and the pursuit of profits. We will not be deceived by so many of our fellow men, we will not be blinded by small changes in form which lack any change in the substance of imperialist expansion. Our suffering has been too long, our sacrifices have been too great, and our human dignity is too strong for us to be prudent any longer.

THE BLACK PANTHER PARTY CALLS FOR FREEDOM AND THE POWER TO DETERMINE OUR DESTINY.
THE BLACK PANTHER PARTY CALLS FOR FULL EMPLOYMENT FOR ALL OUR PEOPLE.

THE BLACK PANTHER PARTY CALLS FOR AN END TO
THE CAPITALIST EXPLOITATION OF OUR COMMU-
NITY.
THE BLACK PANTHER PARTY CALLS FOR DECENT
HOUSING FOR ALL OUR PEOPLE.
THE BLACK PANTHER PARTY CALLS FOR A TRUE
EDUCATION OF OUR PEOPLE.
THE BLACK PANTHER PARTY CALLS FOR EXEMP-
TION FROM MILITARY SERVICE.
THE BLACK PANTHER PARTY CALLS FOR AN END
TO POLICE BRUTALITY.
THE BLACK PANTHER PARTY CALLS FOR FREEDOM
FOR ALL POLITICAL PRISONERS.
THE BLACK PANTHER PARTY CALLS FOR FAIR
TRIALS FOR ALL MEN BY A JURY OF THEIR PEERS.
THE BLACK PANTHER PARTY CALLS FOR A UNITED
NATIONS PLEBISCITE TO DETERMINE THE WILL OF
BLACK PEOPLE AS TO THEIR NATIONAL DESTINY.

Black people and oppressed people in general have lost
faith in the leaders of America, in the government of
America, and in the very structure of American Government (that is, the Constitution, its legal foundation). This
loss of faith is based upon the overwhelming evidence that
this government will not live according to that Constitution
because the Constitution is not designed for its people. For
this reason we assemble a Constitutional Convention to
consider rational and positive alternatives. Alternatives
which will place their emphasis on the common man. Alternatives which will bring about a new economic system in
which the rewards as well as the work will be equally shared
by all people—a Socialist framework in which all groups
will be adequately represented in the decision making and
administration which affects their lives. Alternatives which
will guarantee that all men will attain their full manhood
rights, that they will be able to live, be free, and seek out

those goals which give them respect and dignity while permitting the same privileges for every other man regardless of his condition or status.

The sacredness of man and of the human spirit requires that human dignity and integrity ought to be always respected by every other man. We will settle for nothing less, for at this point in history anything less is but a living death. WE WILL BE FREE and we are here to ordain a new Constitution which will ensure our freedom by enshrining (cherishing) the dignity of the human spirit.

Reply to William Patterson:
September 19, 1970

The excerpts below are from an article by William L. Patterson, Communist Party, U.S.A. They are included here to clarify Huey Newton's reply which follows. Mr. Patterson's article was entitled "The Black Panther Party: A Force Against U.S. Imperialism," and reprinted in the July 4, 1970, issue of the Black Panther newspaper.

PATTERSON:

Emerging in the Fall of 1966 from the most depressed sections of the white police-ridden Black ghetto of Oakland, California, the Black Panther Party for Self-Defense has in a remarkable short time been raised by its leadership to be an extremely significant force in the political battles against American reaction. Frenzied-like imperialist top governmental agents have continuously sought the extermination of the Black Panther leadership and the destruction of its Party.

What social phenomena brought the Black Panther Party into being?

First: police brutality, unrestricted, unrestrained and officially endorsed as constituting "law and order."

Second: Deep emotional and political frustrations brought on by the failure of White labor leadership and liberals among the White masses to recognize not only the validity of the demands of Blacks for equality of rights and opportunities NOW but as well the inseparable relation of those demands to the progressive American political scene. More, exactly how support of those demands would revitalize national morality and check the process of dehumanization initiated by racism.

Third: The consequent political conclusion that Blacks seeking freedom had to go it alone. Plus a determination on the part of Black youth to fight racism in its own way, regardless of the price they might have to pay. This conclusion came from a failure to understand that to save Black, Brown, Red and Yellow Americans from the destructive ravages of genocide the whole of the U.S. has to be saved from the menace of imperialism.

Objective conditions were ripe for the emergence of the Black Panther Party. Its birth, its development, the desperateness of its ideological and political struggles are unique in the annals of the magnificent battles Black Liberation fighters have waged in the U.S.A. before the Civil War against slavery and after. It did not come onto the stage of history as did the NAACP (National Association for the Advancement of Colored People) piloted by the Black middle class and a White liberal bourgeoisie that dictated policy. It came from the very bowels of the ghetto's deprived and harassed youth. These events testify to the fact that the Black Communities, Black ghettos, politically and otherwise warped and stunted in their growth by the foul plague racism has foisted upon them, are fighting fronts that contain unsurpassable reserves for the mounting struggle against imperialism, USA, the fight for peace, a democracy of and for the people, and freedom. The Black Panther Party for Self-Defense was dedicated to the struggle to end murderous police violence. Police violence was rampant in Oakland's Black ghetto. The ruling class had launched a wave of terror against Black citizens. It was fearful of the high tension in the ghetto and sought to quell the democratic struggles for national liberation that seemed imminent.

When this youthful Black leadership moved into the arena of organized political struggle it believed that police terror, if sharply challenged, could readily be brought to an end. It was to find, however, through struggle, that the police were not an independent social force. The police, as the Communist Party had declared, was a terrorist agency of government used to brutalize all who would not passively accept violation of their inalienable and constitutional rights, which included the allies of the "colored" citizenry.

Racism had been pushed to genocidal proportions in Oakland. Large numbers of Blacks had migrated there during World War II from Louisiana, Texas and other points South. The shipbuilding industry gave work to thousands. The end of the war saw thousands ruthlessly thrust jobless into the streets. Peacetime economy can make unlimited jobs. It made jobs, but in the aircraft factories that opened up Blacks were the last to be hired. They were discriminated against in the skilled jobs. Thousands of Blacks found themselves among the unemployed and almost utterly ignored by city, state and Federal governments when relief was considered.

During the war imperialist ideologists had vocally proclaimed that American imperialism was out to destroy the murderous racial practices of the ruling class of the German Reich and smash its leadership. Nazi war criminals who had borrowed heavily from the bestial racist arsenal of America's ruling class were condemned, tried and punished. Justice Robert Jackson, the American prosecutor, had made an outstanding condemnation of bigotry and racism in his opening remarks at Nuremberg's trial. U.S. imperialists and racists had signed the Charter of the United Nations. The Government again formally committed itself to end racism, reaffirming constitutional and legislative pledges its leaders never meant to keep.

Millions of Black Americans were once more deluded. Many believed that the American brand of racism was also to be a victim of the war crimes trial. They did not realize that racism was inherent in capitalism. Nor did they appreciate how deeply racism had penetrated American life. They did not understand the nature or scope of the struggle against it nor did they see it as a struggle for country and mankind as well as for themselves.

Blacks in Oakland, as elsewhere, demanded work or adequate relief. They got neither. The terror that had been slackened during the hot war was now renewed as the cold war was intensified. It was revived with greater consciousness. The bourgeoisie felt the need to smash the natural trend toward unity that had begun to develop as Black and White worked side by side on the war jobs. America's White ideologists began by painting anew the picture of Blacks as a shiftless cowardly people with incurable criminal tendencies. Blacks were terrorists!

The situation in Oakland was worse than in many other places because the war and the depression before it brought an influx of politically backward White Southerners literally steeped in the myths of White superiority. The picture of Blacks painted by ruling class ideologists was acceptable to those Whites now that a new fight for jobs had been sharpened. Labor had done little or nothing to help its rank and file study the complexities of the question of racial persecution.

The leadership of White labor had been bought off or duped by the "Establishment." It ignored the democratic demands of Blacks even though these demands clearly reflected the needs of all of American labor. The political demands advanced by Blacks should have been embraced by labor as it developed as a class for itself. It was wise to sing "We ain't goin study war no more" but wiser not to stop studying . . . the class nature and consequences of racism.

Communists on the West Coast had called for unity in struggle of Black and White. They spoke sharply of the menace of racism to labor. The call though clear was ineffective in the ghetto save around questions of Civil Rights. Reaction had launched a systematic and persistent anti-Communist crusade in the ghetto. It had no little effect because it was picked up by Black middle-class leaders who felt their own organizations challenged by a scientific approach to the struggle.

The leading Black organization on the liberation front, the NAACP, was anti-Communist. It was under the leadership of White philanthropists and their Black sychophants. It was not prepared or able to wage a militant class struggle for the rights of Blacks or for labor's unity with Blacks. The leadership of the Black Panther Party for Self-Defense stepped into what seemed to be a political vacuum.

But a program of self-defense, no matter how militant in and of itself, gets an oppressed people nowhere. The police of an oppressor use force and violence under the direction of business and political leaders who label it "law and order." It is a method of political relationship of the administrative branch of the government with minority groups.

It is to the great credit of the Black Panther leadership that it quickly recognized this structural set-up. The Party's name was changed. "For Self-Defense" was dropped. The organization became THE BLACK PANTHER PARTY. The Party's outlook was broadened. It was now a more effective weapon for self-defense because it sought a line of offensive activities that could, if consistently pursued, put an end to police terror. It now began to see the historical necessity to remove the racist from the seats of power in the economic and political life of the country. That Party had taken a leap forward in its theoretical outlook but by no means had it mastered the science it espoused.

The Black Panther Party called itself a Marxist-guided organization. It made the study of Marxism-Leninism compulsory among the leading cadre. This step was unprecedented in the history of the Black Liberation struggle. The Panthers did not lift the Black Liberation movement to an international level. The Communist Party of the U.S.A. had already done that. That is why it was feared and all progressive steps were charged to it. Black and White Communists had stood in international bodies to proclaim that inseparable relation of the struggle of Blacks in the U.S.A. to the world-wide freedom struggle. The Black Liberation struggle no less needs the guidance of a science than does every other liberation struggle. Social revolution is a science, as the Communists have said many times, a science to be creatively used has to be mastered and the science guiding revolution must of historical necessity be a universal science. That science is Marxism-Leninism.

During the war against slavery, Karl Marx has said that labor in a White skin could not emancipate itself while labor in a Black skin was branded. That axiom still holds true. It reveals the inseparable relationship of labor and national liberation.

For the first time in the history of the Black Liberation struggle an exclusively Black-led political party had sought the aid of science in its leaders' efforts to find a solution to a problem provoked by the avarice, lust and murderous greed of a system of society. Capitalism has divided a powerful segment of mankind along the color line and has dehumanized millions in the process.

To adopt a social science as a guiding line in the struggle for liberation is a far-reaching forward step. Those who are able to take such a step at once become a menace insofar as the exploiter's analysis goes. At the same time, such a group deserves the respect and the serious political attention of all who regard themselves as revolutionists. For that reason the Black Panther Party deserves the closest constructive attention that can be given by all forces in the revolutionary ranks. The vocal espousal of a science and its political and ideological mastery in life are two different matters. It is not difficult to see that the police are not bosses but servants with a license to murder all who fight to put human rights on a plane above that occupied by property rights. After being arrested by the police and given the customary beating, Black Panthers were hailed before the court to get more than a birds-eye view of the capitalist machinery of home warfare before being imprisoned. Confronted by the terror of the Court, before a judge who was a legal despot with control even over the defense counsel who is considered an "officer" of the Court, the Black Panthers did not know how, even with the science of Marxism-Leninism, to effectively strike back. It had not yet learned from others or through experience of its own, the political power of mass action.

There were among the Panthers those who immediately argued that "liberation comes out of the barrel of a gun." Some who argued this were honest but had no serious appreciation of the relation of forces. They were moved by emotionalism—not science. Others were agents whom the Department of Justice had inspired to join the Panthers in order to destroy it, if possible, from within.

There is, of course, an element of Marxist-Leninist truth in the assertion that liberation can come out of the barrel of a gun but its value is determined by the objective situation, the existing relation of forces and not by emotional fervor. A resort to arms does not mechanically apply to all situations simply because it may apply to one. To attempt implementation of the assertion that liberation comes from guns under today's conditions in the U.S.A. is to commit a provocation for which one will pay dearly. The Panthers have learned that neither Black nor White America en masse is ready for the gun as a major instrument of freedom, or for guerrilla warfare, nor for that matter was all of the Black Panther leadership. Those who argued for the provocative step were voted down. But propagation of their anti-Marxist step had left its mark on the organization and its political program. It had been an aid to bloodthirsty Black-hating police and a detriment to Black Panther development and the National Liberation struggle. Instead of clarity, it brought confusion.

There were among the Panthers those who believed that the use of vulgar and obscene language makes the words of a platform or street speaker more effective. For a revolutionary's words are weapons that inspire, ennoble and galvanize into action. They are not something with which to titillate or to arouse to an orgy of passion. Words can alienate, or educate and endear. They can sign people off or on. The Panther top leadership has come out against vulgarity when used for the purpose of securing a laugh or exciting an emotional spasm. But again an alien thesis had been introduced into their generally progressive program of action. These lessons from life are of far-reaching value if seriously studied. They add to the arsenal of liberation struggles.

The weaknesses of the Black Panther Party on the ideological and programmatical fronts are now weaknesses of growth and not of deterioration. However, if not systematically and persistently combated they can lead to deterioration.

It has been asserted by some within the Black Panther Party that "The world of Marxism-Leninism has become a jungle of opinion in which conflicting interpretation from Right revisionism to Left dogmatism, foist off their reactionary and blind philosophies as revolutionary Marxism-Leninism. Around the world and in every nation, people, all who call themselves Marxist-Leninists are at each other's throats." American imperialism seeks to inject this line of thought into the heads of all who seek a scientifically developed program of struggle against its wars, its racism, its persecution of the working class. But one who wishes to be a revolutionary should mark well the centennary of the birth of Vladimir Ilyich Lenin which so recently took place in Moscow to say nothing about studying the theoretical conferences on "Leninism and Contemporaneity" which took place in Prague late in 1969.

Representatives of Marxist-Leninist thought were present from most of the countries of the world. And to the dismay of world imperialism the voices of the representatives of Marxist-Leninist parties of the world were almost as one. Gus Hall, General Secretary of the Communist Party of the U.S.A., speaking in Moscow, said among other things:

"The revisionist opponents of Marxism-Leninism have adopted the typical capitalist tactic of divide and destroy . . . they are out to separate the national liberation struggles from their socialist source of strength . . .

"The attempt is to destroy the teachings of Marx and Lenin. Then separate them and by so doing to destroy the science of Marxism-Leninism . . ." Gus Hall concluded: "On this, the Centennial of Lenin's birth we can confidently say to the vulgar revisionists: your attempts are coming too late in history; your efforts may cause disruption here and there. But the very processes of life and the class struggle have condemned you to failure. Marxism-Leninism is the process of truth. It is indispensable and indestructible." The same can be said to the Left sectarians of whom there are some among the Panthers.

It cannot be denied that the relentless struggle for equality of rights and human dignity pursued by the Black Panthers has both awakened and inspired millions of White youth who, until the emergence of the Panthers, paid little heed to the dehumanizing effects of racism on them or of its effect on national morality.

There are among the leaders of the Panthers those who believe that the United States is already in the throes of fascist terror; they generalize their own experiences. That is wrong. Despite the fascist-like nature of the terror from which Black nationals have suffered for a century and the fascist-like racist terror now rampant, the possibilities that remain openly to fight for the completion of the bourgeois revolution and its tranference into a Socialist revolution offers irrefutable proof that this position that fascism dominates the American scene is not consistent with reality. The Court's reversal of the vicious decision that had sent Huey Newton, a founder of the Panther Party, to prison, is also proof that the trend toward fascism in the U.S.A. can successfully be fought.

Propagation of the idea of existing fascism can only weaken the struggle to destroy fascist trends, and the development of an anti-fascist coalition. As has been said in the introduction to the New Program of the Communist Party, U.S.A.:

"Wherever one looks, there is struggle in the United States today. People are on the march. More and more are engaged in struggles for peace, for Black and Brown liberation, for economic advancement. More and more are seeking fundamental solution. There is radicalization. . . ."

We will fight increasingly for the constitutional rights of the Black Panther Party for we know that:

"Through immediate struggle workers organize and learn the need to battle further. They learn who the enemy is and how to fight ultimately to the socialist revolution . . .

"Class consciousness begins with recognition of the fundamental community interests of Black and White workers.

The Black Panther Party is in the process of growth and development at a moment when the anti-imperialist struggle sharpens and deepens. It is on a vital front of that struggle. History demands that all aid to overcome its weaknesses of growth shall be forthcoming. The position of the Communist Party U.S.A. is in support of history. A wide diversity of views exists on the American Left. We are internationalist with an awareness that the Black Liberation struggle is of vital significance to the world revolutionary movement. More constructive aid must be given to the Black Panther Party.

A broad Black Liberation Front, including all forces opposed to racism and genocidal policies and practices of American imperialism, must be created. It should be composed of Black, Brown, Red, Yellow and White forces and form a coalition confronting warmongers and racists at all crisis points. The Communists must play a leading role in the development of this coalition.

NEWTON:

When Mr. Patterson discusses the social phenomena that brought the Party into being, he makes no mention of the primary aspect: the economic exploitation of Blacks. His conception that the Party was primarily a self-defense group against police brutality is a most narrow interpretation of the concept of self-defense by the oppressed masses. He also seems to have no understanding of the historical predecessors of the Party, especially Malcolm. He fails to understand the lessons learned by the Party through the failures of such civil-rights organizations as SNCC, NAACP, etc. (i.e. power politics, mass force). Mr. Patterson questions whether Blacks should have their own organization to fight for national liberation. While he often says the struggle is for national liberation he really does not believe that Blacks in the U.S. are a colony. He says Blacks made a mistake when they decided that they had to control and lead the fight for their liberation and freedom. He talks about "the price they might have to pay." Does he propose that Blacks wait for White labor to lead the liberation struggle at a time when White labor subjectively views itself as a beneficiary of capitalism? Labor unions are presently stooges of the capitalist warmongers. In an attempt to label the Party as nationalist (that is, not interested in the struggles of people of other races) he completely fails to understand that *our freedom and dignity is necessarily tied to the freedom and dignity of the oppressed masses of the world.*

Mr. Patterson never specifies what he means when he talks about the desperateness of the Party's ideological and political struggles. Were they "desperate" or merely intense, as we sought to confront the enemy and move the struggle to a higher level? What does Patterson mean when he refers to Blacks as "reserves" in the fight against imperialism? If Blacks are the "reserves" then who is the forefront of the struggle? It is apparent to any sane person that Blacks are the vanguard of the struggle against imperialism in the U.S.

Patterson tries to make the people think that the B.P.P. thought that police terror could be "readily brought to an end" if it was "sharply challenged." This ties in with his earlier notion that the Party was organized by fools who were just reacting on a gut level to the police brutality they had seen all around them. He forgets or dismisses all of my early writings and all of Eldridge Cleaver's early writings about who the police are, and implies that the Party did not understand that the pigs are an agent of the ruling class. I wrote in "Functional Definition of Politics" (while the Party was still the B.P.P. for Self-Defense) that "police are an occupying army." I further stated that "there is a great similarity between the occupying army in Southeast Asia and the occupation of our communities by the racist police. The armies are there not to protect the people of South Vietnam, but to brutalize and oppress them for the interests of the selfish imperial power." Or Eldridge from *Soul On Ice:* "The police department and the armed forces are the two arms of the power structure, the muscles of control and enforcement . . . they use force to make you do what the deciders have decided you must do . . . Both police and armed forces follow orders. Orders flow from the top down." Patterson will not admit that the Panther Party leadership understood this relationship from the very beginning because he is a revisionist and opposed to armed struggle. He tries to hide my major point in the article on "Functional Definition of Politics" because he does not want to meet those arguments head-on. The Black Panther Party picked up the gun and concentrated on Point 7 of the program because in this way we could most clearly communicate to the Black community the necessity of picking up the gun to gain liberation and freedom. It was not because we could end police terror merely by "sharply challenging" the police. This of course is not to say that by challenging the police the Party did not begin to show that if a few people with guns challenged the police they could have some effect, but it was done in the context of educating the masses of the potential power of an armed Black community. Our program is an attack upon U.S. imperialism in all its forms and faces. We have used the police as a catalyst because the people on the bottom of the bottom are most affected by that government agency. We call it a government agency because the police act like a government in our community. We realize that the police departments are arms of the decision makers who tell their unleashed dogs whom and when to kill. This is true of the military as well as the police. The Vietnamese who are fighting the military realize that the military is but a foot soldier with a decision maker behind him; nevertheless, the military exists and is reckoned with in an appropriate manner. The police are the foot soldiers in our community and that is why the Vietnamese people call for American people to unite and topple the reactionary regime in this country in order to win their fight for liberation.

We call upon the people of the world to struggle with us (which they are doing) to topple imperialism so that we'll become free from the local evil gentry and corrupt officials.

This is all the way up the line from the foot soldier to his master somewhere in Standard Oil, General Motors, Bell Telephone, Chrysler Motors, etc. We do not even acknowledge the electoral administrative civil government because we realize they're only puppets of the avaricious businessmen.

Patterson's comment about the bourgeoisie needing to smash the natural trend of unity that was developing between Black and White workers is crap. What evidence can he present of this upsurge under imperialism. Do White workers independently of vanguard leadership and Black struggle automatically begin to see common interests with Black workers? Did the ruling class really have to begin anew to paint racist conceptions of Blacks? Did these conceptions ever stop? This whole position seems to be a cover-up to justify the CP's position on World War II and Roosevelt.

He tries to explain the Party with some brand of Oakland particularism. As if the oppression was not as great or greater elsewhere in the large Black ghettos in Chicago, New York, Boston, Newark, etc. This is actually a cover to say that Southern workers were more racist than their Northern counterparts. As if racism is not rampant all over the country. As if our native-grown racists in California are not every bit as vicious as the ones from the South. It was Malcolm who pointed out that the Mason-Dixon line was at the Canadian border.

The Party never had a program of self-defense in the sense that Patterson speaks of. He fails to understand that the Party wanted to explain and demonstrate that political power grows out of the barrel of a gun.

He gets hung-up on the formalism of changing the name of the Party as if that represented a broadening of the Party's views. He does not understand the conception of self-defense that the Black Panther Party originally formulated. When we used "for Self-Defense" we realized that all oppressed people or legitimate revolutionary oppressed people never are the aggressors; all of their action is in self-defense. The Vietnamese people are merely using self-defense; it's the capitalistic, imperialistic exploiters who initiate violence and aggression. So whatever the people do for their liberation, for their freedom, is a self-defense tactic. When we use self-defense, we use it in the broadest sense. We've expressed time and time again, that when we used the words "Self-Defense," it also meant defending ourselves against poor medical care, against unemployment, against poor housing and all the other things that poor and oppressed people of the world suffer. How else can it be explained that even while the Party was the Black Panther Party for Self-Defense that we had the same Ten-Point platform and program that we have to this day.

What we have to do is find out what will mobilize the people. I think the Black Panther Party has done more in three years to mobilize the masses than the American Communist Party has in twenty years. I challenge the Communist Party's claim that they "prepared the way for the people." The U.S. Government, except for a brief period, has not taken the American Communist Party seriously; and the people have not been considered at all. That is precisely why the Communist Party members in the U.S.A. have not been jailed and murdered in large numbers. I think that in the whole history of the Communist Party in the U.S.A., only about five or six people have been incarcerated for a lengthy period. Is this what leads Mr. Patterson to believe the Communist Party has done everything right? This is not what Chairman Mao teaches us. Chairman Mao tells us, "When the enemy strikes out at you blindly, crushing you left and right if he possibly can, then you know you're doing everything right." So I would charge the Communist Party with having been no threat. And they have done something wrong, because they have not been crucified as the enemy is attempting to crucify us.

But of course Mr. Patterson thinks it is the other way around. I think it is because his bourgeois ideology lets him see things through a bourgeois perspective. He claims that because our line is so provocative it has given the established order an excuse to kill us. Well, what excuse have the Vietnamese people given them? I say the only reason the Communist Party's members have not been strung up by their toes is simply because the Communist Party is no threat to this country—not with the classical line they are teaching. They have not captured the imagination of the people, and as far as laying down a foundation for us, we find the road so rocky until we are sure that no one has cleared the way. If they had cleared the way we would have smooth sailing now because they have had thirty years in which to do it.

Patterson says that "the Panthers have learned that neither Black nor White American masses are ready for the gun as a major instrument of freedom, or for guerrilla warfare, nor for that matter was all of the Panther leadership." I agree with him; apparently everyone is not ready for the gun. But I would also ask does he mean we should stop talking about the gun? Should we stop defending ourselves? Is he saying the gun is not a catalyst for oppressed people? Is he saying that the gun is not a tool that we will eventually have to use? Should it not be introduced to the people? If his answer to these questions is affirmative then it follows that the Communist Party of the U.S.A. should drop its Marxist-Leninist line (for which the masses are evidently not ready) and start a new line. And I suppose their new line would be the bourgeoisie democratic electoral politics line which the American Communist Party has embraced. I see very little difference between their line and the Democratic Party's line, both of which are archaic and ready for their positions in the museum.

THE THIRD WORLD

To the National Liberation Front of South Vietnam: August 29, 1970

In the spirit of international revolutionary solidarity the Black Panther Party hereby offers to the National Liberation Front and Provisional Revolutionary Government of South Vietnam an undetermined number of troops to assist you in your fight against American imperialism. It is appropriate for the Black Panther Party to take this action at this time in recognition of the fact that your struggle is also our struggle, for we recognize that our common enemy is the American imperialist who is the leader of international bourgeois domination. There is not one fascist or reactionary government in the world today that could stand without the support of United States imperialism. Therefore our problem is international, and we offer these troops in recognition of the necessity for international alliances to deal with this problem.

Such alliances will advance the struggle toward the final act of dealing with American imperialism. The Black Panther Party views the United States as the "city" of the world, while we view the nations of Africa, Asia and Latin America as the "countryside" of the world. The developing countries are like the Sierra Maestra in Cuba and the United States is like Havana. We note that in Cuba the people's army set up bases in the Sierra Maestra and choked off Havana because it was dependent upon the raw materials of the countryside. After they won all the battles in this countryside the last and final act was for the people to march upon Havana.

The Black Panther Party believes that the revolutionary process will operate in a similar fashion on an international level. A small ruling circle of seventy-six major companies controls the American economy. This elite not only exploits and oppresses Black people within the United States; they are exploiting and oppressing everyone in the world because of the overdeveloped nature of capitalism. Having expanded industry within the United States until it can grow no more, and depleting the raw materials of this nation, they have run amuck abroad in their attempts to extend their economic domination. To end this oppression we must liberate the developing nation—the countryside of the world—and then our final act will be the strike against the "city." As one nation is liberated elsewhere it gives us a better chance to be free here.

The Black Panther Party recognizes that we have certain national problems confined to the continental United States, but we are also aware that while our oppressor has domestic problems these do not stop him from oppressing people all over the world. Therefore we will keep fighting and resisting within the "city" so as to cause as much turmoil as possible and aid our brothers by dividing the troops of the ruling circle.

The Black Panther Party offers these troops because *we are the vanguard party of revolutionary internationalists who give up all claim to nationalism.* We take this position because the United States has acted in a very chauvinistic manner and lost its claim to nationalism. *The United States is an empire which has raped the world to build its wealth here. Therefore the United States is not a nation.* It is a government of international capitalists and inasmuch as they have exploited the world to accumulate wealth this country belongs to the world. The Black Panther Party contends that the United States lost its right to claim nationhood when it used its nationalism as a chauvinistic base to become an empire.

On the other hand, the developing countries have every right to claim nationhood, because they have not exploited anyone. The nationalism of which they speak is simply their rightful claim to autonomy, self-determination and a liberated base from which to fight the international bourgeoisie.

The Black Panther Party supports the claim to nationhood of the developing countries and we embrace their struggle from our position as revolutionary internationalists. We cannot be nationalists when our country is not a nation but an empire. We contend that it is time to open the gates of this country and share the technological knowledge and wealth with the peoples of the world.

History has bestowed upon the Black Panther Party the obligation to take these steps and thereby advance Marxism-Leninism to an even higher level along the path to a socialist state, and then a non-state. This obligation springs both from the dialectical forces in operation at this time and our history as an oppressed Black colony. The fact that our ancestors were kidnapped and forced to come to the United States has destroyed our feeling of nationhood. Because our long cultural heritage was broken we have come to rely less on our history for guidance, and seek our guidance from the future. Everything we do is based upon functionalism and pragmatism, and because we look to the future for salvation we are in a position to become the most progressive and dynamic people on the earth, constantly in motion and progressing, rather than becoming stagnated by the bonds of the past.

Taking these things under consideration, it is no accident

that the vanguard party—without chauvinism or a sense of nationhood—should be the Black Panther Party. Our struggle for liberation is based upon justice and equality for all men. Thus we are interested in the people of any territory where the crack of the oppressor's whip may be heard. We have the historical obligation to take the concept of internationalism to its final conclusion—the destruction of statehood itself. This will lead us into the era where the withering away of the state will occur and men will extend their hand in friendship throughout the world.

This is the world view of the Black Panther Party and in the spirit of revolutionary internationalism, solidarity and friendship we offer these troops to the National Liberation Front and Provisional Government of South Vietnam, and to the people of the world.

Letter From Nguyen Thi Dinh:
October 31, 1970

To: Mr. Huey P. Newton
     Minister of Defense
     Black Panther Party

Dear Comrade:

We are deeply moved by your letter informing us that the Black Panther Party is intending to send to the National Liberation Front and the Provisional Revolutionary Government of the Republic of South Vietnam an undetermined number of troops, assisting us in our struggle against the U.S. imperialist aggressors.

This news was communicated to all the cadres and fighters of the PLAF in South Vietnam; and all of us are delighted to get more comrades-in-arms, so brave as you, on the very soil of the United States.

On behalf of the cadres and fighters of the SVN PLAF I would welcome your noble deed and convey to you our sincere thanks for your warm support to our struggle against U.S. aggression for national salvation. We consider it as a great contribution from your side, an important event of the peace and democratic movement in the United States giving us active support, a friendly gesture voicing your determination to fight side-by-side with the South Vietnamese people for the victory of the common cause of revolution.

In the spirit of international solidarity, you have put forward your responsibility towards history, towards the necessity of uniting actions, sharing joys and sorrows, participating in the struggle against U.S. imperialism.

You have highly appreciated the close relation between our both uncompromising struggles against U.S. imperialism, our common enemy. It is well known now that the U.S. government is the most warlike, not only oppresses and exploits the American people, especially the Black and the coloured ones, but also oppresses and exploits various peoples the world over by all means, irrespective of morality and justice. They have the hunger of dollars and profits which they deprived by the most barbarous ways, including genocide, as they have acted for years in South Vietnam.

In the past years, your just struggle in the U.S. has stimulated us to strengthen unity, and rush forward toward bigger successes.

The U.S. imperialists, although driven by the South Vietnamese and Indochinese people in a defeated position, still have not given up their evil design, still seek to gain the military victories and to negotiate on the position of strength. On the SVN battle-fields, they are actively realizing their policy of "Vietnamization" of the war with a view to maintaining the neocolonialism in South Vietnam and prolonging the partition of our country.

The very nature of the policy of "Vietnamization" is prolonging indefinitely the aggressive war at a degree ever so cruel and barbarous. While Nixon puts forward his "initiative for peace," in SVN the aggressive war got harder and harder; after the "urgent pacification" came the "Eagle campaign"; after that, by the "special pacification" in the countrysides and the "for the people" campaign in the towns, Nixon and the Thieu Ky Khiem clique have perpetrated innumerable barbarous crimes towards the people of all strata in SVN.

The 5 point proposal of Mr. Nixon, put forth on October 7th exposes more clearly his stubborn, perfidious and deceitful nature to U.S. and world opinion. It is clear that Nixon is unwilling to accept a peaceful settlement on the Vietnam problem, but tries to stick to South Vietnam as a neocolony and U.S. military base, as well as to legalize the U.S. aggression in Indochina as a whole.

The U.S. government must seriously respond to the September 17th statement of the RSVN PRG, for it is the just basis, the reasonable and logical solution of the SVN problem. These are also the urgent aspirations of the whole Vietnamese people, of the progressive Americans and of those the world over who cherish peace, freedom and justice.

Dear Comrades, our struggle yet faces a lot of hardships, but we are determined to overcome all difficulties, unite with all progressive forces, to heighten our revolutionary vigilance, to persist in our struggle, resolutely to fight and win. We are sure to win complete victory.

So are our thinkings: At present, the struggles, right in the United States or on the SVN battle-fields, are both making positive contributions for national liberation and safeguarding the world peace. Therefore, your persistent and ever-developing struggle is the most active support to our resistance against U.S. aggression for national salvation.

With profound gratitude, we take notice of your enthusiastic proposal; when necessary, we shall call for your volunteers to assist us.

We are firmly confident that your just cause will enjoy sympathy, warm and strong support of the people at home and abroad, and will win complete victory; and our ever closer coordinated struggle surely stop the bloody hands of the U.S. imperialists and surely contribute winning independence, freedom, democracy and genuine peace.

Best greetings for "unity, militancy, and victory" from the SVN people's liberation fighters.

NGUYEN THI DINH,
Deputy Commander
Of the SVN People's
Liberation Armed Forces.
Republic of South Vietnam

Reply to Roy Wilkins re: Vietnam: September 26, 1970

ROY WILKINS:

Negro Americans who celebrated the release of Huey Newton, co-founder of the Black Panther Party, from a California prison, had their jubilation doused in cold water by Newton's first interview.

He announced that his No. 1 priority was the recruiting of a Black American unit to fight with the National Liberation Front. He wants to help the Viet Cong in Indochina, not with street rallies, parades and hot rhetoric here in the United States, but with guns in the hands of a fighting unit in Vietnam.

If the rank and file Negro Americans expected anything from the Panther leader that would aid them in their daily problems, they were disappointed. But Black Americans have had so many disappointments that they have become cynical. Some of them thought Huey was railroaded to prison just as some of them believe that the Black Panthers are being hounded and killed by the authorities. Accordingly, they were glad of the legal technicality that freed him. It was a victory of sorts over the system.

But what did Huey think about during his nearly two years in custody? The Viet Cong may be hurting, but nothing like the hurting of John Q. Black American. Is a young Black American, as smart and as articulate as Huey Newton, so overcome with the anguish of a people 9,000 miles from the United States that he downgrades the suffering of his own people in the slums of Los Angeles or in the shacks in rural Alabama?

Of course, Huey knows about this suffering. It was the resentment over this treatment that led, at least in part, to the founding of the Black Panthers. But Huey, for all his talents, is also a revolutionary. Revolutionaries get confused. They think that following a "line" is more important than winning an improvement for their people. They are worried about keeping straight with some revolutionary leader in a far country. They are moved but little by the plight of Black Americans cooped up on Indiana Avenue in Chicago or on Auburn Avenue in Atlanta.

What about the Black migrant workers in New Jersey, Pennsylvania and New York who need smart and dedicated Huey Newtons to help them out of the misery of their camps? And there are the nearly two million Black public school children who are being crippled for life in the inferior school systems perpetrated by politicians who are juggling desegregation and quality education.

Huey should know that the Black people of Washington, D.C., the nation's capital, are holed up in their homes each night, terror stricken over robberies, rapes and murder. In all cities, big and little, coalitions and officials and just plain Black citizens are battling for jobs and paychecks.

They need low-income housing in suburbs. Mississippi has just reapportioned several districts and wants to reduce the Black vote by requiring re-registration. In short, as the late Bert Williams, the Black comedian, once said, "we need everything from an overcoat in."

In this state, a Newton top priority plan for a company of Black American soldiers to fight for the Viet Cong generates only damp enthusiasm. Newton, an attractive and personable young man, is described in one news dispatch as being the darling of White revolutionaries. It figures.

NEWTON:

It is clear that your published criticism of my statement regarding the commitment of Black Panthers to the revolutionary struggle of the National Liberation Front in Vietnam was written for the comfort and aid of the oppressors in this nation rather than for the oppressed. I want to take this opportunity to make my intent clear to the oppressed of this wretched land.

I am very grateful for the support and encouragement I received from many thousands of Black people during my thirty-three months in prison. I always found the reports of their faith and confidence in me, and their wish to see me free to be of great sources of strength during that sojourn (to live for a while). My release was a joyous event for me and the people, and I thank them for freeing me.

I am also aware that the enemies of the people—the ruling circle of America—are just as anxious to see me dead or in prison and will go to any lengths to accomplish their evil purpose. This is not because of me but because of the goals and the ideology of the Black Panther Party, a vanguard party totally committed to the liberation of those Blacks who have been missed by almost every program and legislative change resulting from the Civil-Rights Movement.

Your statement charging me with "wrong priorities" reflects your own self-interest as a so-called leader of Blacks who has the ear of the ruling circle, and your obvious class interests and identification with the ruling circle. Your insidious "White baiting" is also a reflection of self-interest, lack of understanding, and incipient Black racism. Should you continue such attacks for the benefit of the oppressor, you will only reveal yourself to be a treacherous enemy of the people who mislead them by placing self-interest above the objective needs and interests of the Black lumpenproletariat—America's wretched of the earth.

We recognize, and many Blacks with us, that the civil-rights laws which you have won in the recent past have not protected the people, but have frustrated their drive toward freedom. Even though recognizing this, some Blacks continue to put their faith in you because they feel it necessary to hang on to the belief that America will transform itself through its own legal mechanisms. This does not make sense, for the numerous cases you cite throughout the land are evidence to the contrary. A people who have needed "everything from an overcoat in" for literally centuries cannot objectively expect their oppressors to "heal themselves." There is obviously some deeper motivation for the oppression, motivation not only based on the character of the oppressors, but upon the fundamental aspects of the American system itself. Yet we all seem to have some need for dreams of self-healing.

The Black Panther Party puts the struggle on such a level and gives analyses and answers to this madness so that it is no longer necessary for the people to accept a dream. We encourage the people to strive for real goals: survival, liberation, and freedom.

The priorities of the Black Panther Party are in full view of all Black people in this land. Our first priority is survival and we place this in the context of the needs of the people. Therefore our programs have helped people to survive through Breakfast for School Children, Health Clinics, and newly developing programs such as Free Clothing, Free Shoes, Loans to Welfare Mothers, Free Buses to Prisons for Families of Inmates. The people have rallied to these programs because they meet their basic and daily needs. The priorities of the Black Panther Party are well stated in our Ten-Point Program which is published weekly in our paper.

We recognize that our oppression is supported and maintained by the fire power utilized by the agents of the omnipotent administrators. We recognize that the small ruling class which exploits us here finds it to their economic advantage to exploit the people of distant lands. We recognize that America is no longer a nation but an empire, and the same troops who occupy and kill at Jackson State, Birmingham, Chicago and New Orleans are also occupying and killing in My Lai, in Phnom Penh and many other places. The same ruling class which controls the military and government here also controls the military and government in South Vietnam and Cambodia.

America is World-Enemy-Number-One and the military is its strong arm. We feel that it is imperative (necessary) to defend people of color when they are attacked by American troops in other lands. These attacks are designed to continue the profit-mongering of the ruling class and their carbon lackeys.

Black people in America have long been affected in a negative way by America's war of imperialism. The Black Panther Party now understands what is going on and is moving to develop appropriate responses. We are internationalists because our struggle must proceed on many fronts. While we feed and clothe the poor at home we must meet and attack the oppressor wherever he may be found.

It is clear, however, that you are also an internationalist, but in support of imperialism and at the expense of Black people who contribute so much to you. Recently you signed a full-page advertisement in the *New York Times* urging this government to send jets to Israel. We challenge you to show the people how your support of this ad is designed to improve their lot rather than your own self-interests. That advertisement cost several thousand dollars of somebody's money which could have been put to good use by those very Black people you accuse me of ignoring. Why do you support imperialism and ignore the reality which indicates so clearly that the lowly conditions of Blacks are caused by a complex intermingling of capitalism, imperialism and racism? All of these must be dealt with at the same time if we are to end our oppression.

I am sorry you felt the need to attack me and that this response must be made. We will be free and we will settle for nothing less. Our number-one priority is survival of Black people in this land, and we will use all necessary and sufficient means to do so.

On the Middle East:
September 5, 1970

DAVID*: The press conference was called in response to the allegations that the Black Panther Party had a delegation of Panther members led by Stokely Carmichael in Jordan. The Minister of Defense, Huey P. Newton, is here to repudiate those statements because we do not have any Panthers in Jordan; but we do have an international section in Algeria headed by the Minister of Information, Eldridge Cleaver, and our Field Marshal, Donald Cox. They are representatives of our Party who are in daily contact with the Palestinian Liberation organization, and they're the only authorized Panthers outside of the United States of America.

NEWTON: We further charge that Stokely Carmichael is operating as an agent of the CIA. We have no proof of this but we have some evidence. His actions are speaking for themselves. We notice that when the House of Un-American Activities (HUAC) investigated the Black Panther Party, Stokely Carmichael, shortly after or during the investigation, came out with a statement that the Party was dishonest. He also made other charges that were not based upon fact. When he was approached about this he said that perhaps he was untimely in his charge, and that he was sorry about this. We further charge that he's in cahoots with his wife Miriam Makeba who is also an agent. And as I said before we have no proof, but Stokely Carmichael's behavior infers that he is an agent. Now we hear through the wire

* David Hilliard, Chief of Staff of the Black Panther Party.

and through our embassy in Algiers that Stokely Carmichael is leading a delegation of eighteen Party members in
Jordan against the Jewish people to promote the Palestin-
ians and the interest of the Black Power movement. As a
matter of fact, "Black Power" movement was mentioned on
this wire. As you very well know, the Black Panther Party
does not subscribe to "Black Power" as such. Not the
"Black Power" that has been defined by Stokely Carmichael
and Nixon. They seem to agree upon the stipulated definition of "Black Power" which is no more than Black capitalism. That definition is reactionary and certainly not a
philosophy that would meet the interest of the people. It
would only support the interest of a small group of people.
Stokely Carmichael has further stated that Pan-Africanism
is the highest expression of "Black Power." We say that Pan-
Africanism is the highest expression of cultural nationalism.
The Black Panther Party is internationalist.

We realize that most of the African governments who
adhere to the philosophy of Pan-Africanism are also
aligned with United States imperialism. In other words,
these governments are saying that if the United States will
let us exist as a class to oppress our African people then we
will cooperate; in other words, Black oppressing Black.
This is Stokely Carmichael's philosophy. It is also the philosophy of some of the reactionary governments in Africa.

We would like to emphasize that we support the people
of Africa in their struggle against imperialism, and that our
statements do not affect this comradely love that we have
for all people in the world who are struggling against
United States imperialism. We know that without the support of United States imperialism no reactionary government can exist. So we are very careful when we start
supporting a government that has relationships in support
of the United States.

And now there is this very strange incident of Stokely
Carmichael's allegedly leading a delegation of Black

Panthers—the same Stokely Carmichael who denounced the Party a short time ago. He said that socialism is not the question, economics is not the question, but it is entirely a question of racism. We take issue with this; we realize that the United States is a racist country, but we also realize the roots of the racism, and the roots of the racism is based upon the profit motive and capitalism. So we would like to start with the cause and then later on handle its effects.

We believe that while socialism will not wipe out racism completely, a foundation will be laid. When we change the structure of bourgeoisie society; when we transform the structure into a socialist society, then we're one step toward changing attitudes. The people then will have control of the mass media, radio, television, newspapers, and these are part of the mechanisms that shape attitudes. We know that the concept of cultural lag will probably run true to form. While the structure changes the attitudes will lag behind because values take some time to change. But we say that the only way to start changing the racist nature of the society is to revolutionize or transform the institutions. So we would like to reiterate our support for the Palestinian people.

We would like to make it very clear that the Black Panther Party is not anti-Semitic. We've been charged with being anti-Semitic. As a matter of fact, statements could be cited where some member of the Party has made some statements in anger to hurt some of our White radical friends because we believed that they did not live up to the friendship agreement. But these were internal fights. They should have been kept internal, but they were exposed and used by the reactionaries, and this was partially our fault because we indulged in that. But as far as our official position, we are not anti-Semitic. As far as the Israeli people are concerned we are not against the Jewish people. We are against that government that will persecute the Palestinian people. We have to admit that there is something wrong in the Middle East. The Palestinian people are living in hovels, they don't have a land, they've been stripped and murdered; and we cannot support this for any reason. We also realize some of the shortcomings of the United Arab Republic. Our view is that the people led by the Palestinian people should be led into a struggle, a revolutionary struggle in order to transform the Middle East into truly a peoples' republic. And at the same time we support a small group of people who are in Israel who are revolutionary and working to see that the Zionist government of Israel is transformed into a secular peoples' state instead of a religious state.

We say that the way the country is operating at this time is the height of chauvinism and ethnocentrism. I say this because any state that requires its members to adhere to a certain religion is a reactionary state. We must transform the world into a place where people can live. We are chiefly interested in the survival of our people, but not at the expense of other people.

Black people in America have been persecuted; therefore it is easy for us to identify with other people who are suffering. We have a long history of being enslaved and murdered. We have wrestled with the question of nationalism and we have concluded that we have a moral right to embrace nationalism. We have a moral right to choose separatism, to move into a separate state just as the Jewish people have that moral right. But we realize that United States imperialism will not allow us to separate and live side-by-side with United States imperialism. It's obvious that we could not become self-determined because the United States will not let countries exist 15 million miles away in freedom. They will not let these countries exist in freedom 15 million miles away so they certainly will not let us exist in a separate state in North America in freedom. So the question can be put into the future.

The first task is to transform society so the people can

live in freedom. Our central task is to overthrow the ruling circle, who will not permit self-determination to exist in the world. After we achieve this goal the question of nationalism can be handled. Black nationalists could then go to the U.N. and ask for a plebiscite in order to ask the people which way they want to go. After transformation into a socialist society, there may be no need for separation. This transformation can only take place by wiping out United States imperialism and establishing a new earth, a new society, and a new world. So politically and strategically the correct action to take is not separation but world revolution in order to wipe out imperialism. Then people will be free to decide their destiny. Self-determination and national independence cannot really exist while United States imperialism is alive. That is why we don't support nationalism as our goal. In some instances we might support nationalism as a strategy; we call this revolutionary nationalism. The motives are internationalist because the revolutionaries are attempting to secure liberated territory in order to choke imperialism by cutting them off from the countryside. When the motive for national liberation is solely to create a capitalist state so that the ruling circle of that capitalist state can align itself with United States imperialism, then it is reactionary nationalism, and it cannot be supported by revolutionaries.

Israel was created by Western imperialism and maintained by Western fire power. The Jewish people have a right to exist as long as they solely exist to down the reactionary expansionist Israeli Government. Our situation is similar in so many ways; we say, that morally perhaps, the Jewish people can make a case for separatism and a Zionist state based upon their religion for self-defense. We say, morally, perhaps we could accept this, but politically and strategically we know that it is incorrect. In the first place it is perpetuating nationalism; perpetuating reaction, if nationalism is reaction, and I think that the United States proves this by using nationalism to rape the world and dominate everyone else. In other words, it went from nationalism to the natural conclusion which is empire or imperialism. So the Jewish people must be careful not to be an agent of imperialism. We are asking the progressive forces, the revolutionary forces inside of Israel, to transform that society so that the people of the Moslem religion, the people of the Jewish religion, the people who live in the Middle East, will be able to come together as one man and truly build a new world. As a matter of fact, we are looking forward to this time, and we see that this time will exist; we see the contradiction that's developing between the Palestinian people and the UAR. We also see a growing group inside of Israel that is organizing against the racist tactics of the Israeli Government. I say that if we go over the record we can see where the Jewish students demonstrated against their Minister of Defense, against the war tactics of Israel; and we encourage this activity, we struggle with this group of the Jewish people. So we reject any charges of being anti-Semitic. We realize that some people who happen to be Jewish and who support Israel will use the Black Panther Party's position that is against imperialism and against the agents of the imperialist as an attack of anti-Semitism. We think that this is a back-biting, racist, underhanded tactic and we will treat it as such. We have respect for all people, and we have respect for the right for any people to exist. So we want the Jewish people and the Palestinian people to live in harmony together. We support the Palestinian's just struggle for liberation one hundred percent. We will go on doing this, and we would like for all of the progressive people of the world to join in our ranks in order to make a world in which all people can live.

Repression Breeds Resistance:
January 16, 1970

SECHABA*: Mr. Newton, welcome back from jail and thank you for granting us this interview. First we would like you to explain the relationship between the Black Panther Party and the Black Power movement.

NEWTON: The Black Panther Party grew out of the Black Power movement, but the Party transformed the ideology of Black Power into a socialist ideology, a Marxist-Leninist ideology. The Black Power movement has a tendency to have a capitalistic orientation along the lines of Marcus Garvey's program and the kind of organization that Elijah Muhammed has. The Black Panther Party feels that not even the Black bourgeoisie will be able to compete with imperialism, whose central base is here in North America. The United States is the central base of the bourgeoisie, and this is because this country is really not a nation any longer, but an empire that controls the world through economics and physical force—military might. The Black Panther Party has transformed this movement into a socialist movement and we have become not nationalists, like the Black Power movement in the past, but internationalists.

The bourgeoisie that is based here in America has an international character because it exploits the world, it

---

* *Sechaba* is the official organ of the African National Congress of South Africa, a liberation party which, having been banned in South Africa, operates in exile. This interview was arranged by the Africa Research Group with the assistance of Karen Wald, and took place in Berkeley within a week of Huey Newton's release from a three-year jail term.

controls the wealth of the world; it has stolen, usurped, the wealth of the people of the world, including the people who are in the Black colony here in America and who were stolen from Africa. We feel that the only way that we can combat an international enemy is through an international strategy of unity of all exploited people who will overthrow the international bourgeoisie and replace it with a dictatorship by the proletariat, the workers of the world. And we feel that after imperialism is destroyed, nationhood will no longer be necessary, for the state will then wither away. Then the whole world will belong to the people and the old national boundary lines will no longer exist. We think that the movement is at this stage; we think that the dialectics are now on the verge of taking socialism, social ideology, to its final goal: communism and the absence of statehood.

SECHABA: Do you want to say a little about the program of action in the immediate future for the Party and for yourself?

NEWTON: Our program is armed struggle. We have hooked up with the people who are rising up all over the world with arms because we feel that only with the power of the gun will the bourgeoisie be destroyed and the world transformed. We feel that the imperialists will not become Buddhists overnight; they will not lay down their butcher knives. Therefore, the people will have to use certain measures to restore peace to the world and to restrain the madmen who are running amuck throughout the world and oppressing people everywhere. The World-Enemy-Number-One is the ruling circle in the United States of America. We view the United States as the "city" of the world and all the other countries as a "countryside."

As one country becomes free, it makes each country stronger because it develops a base of liberated territory so that we'll be in a better strategic position to fight, and also it will be one step toward cutting off the raw materials that imperialism needs to feed its factories here at home. We will slowly strangle imperialism by freeing one country after another. This is why we support the brothers and sisters in Southern and Northern Africa as well as those in Asia and Latin America who are struggling against capitalism and imperialism, for socialistic goals. We support all struggles where people are struggling for freedom, and we also support our European brothers and sisters who are struggling to overthrow the bourgeoisie in their country. While we are not nationalists, we support national wars of independence because this is a step again towards cutting off the international bourgeoisie which is based in the United States. We feel that every country has a right to be nationalistic to a point, as long as they are internationalists at the same time. We feel that Black people in America have a moral right to claim nationhood because we are a colonized people. But history won't allow us to claim nationhood. We must take socialist development to its final stage to rid the world of the imperialist threat—the threat of the capitalist and the warmonger. Once America is destroyed then there will be no need for nationhood because the nations will no longer need to defend themselves against imperialism, for this is the most powerful imperialist country in the world, and other imperialist countries depend on the backing of the U.S. At this point the imperialist is running rampant. Therefore any country has a right to claim nationhood or be nationalist as long as they are internationalists as well.

If they are only nationalist then they are chauvinist. If they are both nationalist and internationalist they realize that they need liberated territory, but they also realize that their interests are the same as every other people's interest who are fighting against imperialism. While we respect your fight for nationhood and independence, and we struggle with you, we feel that we must destroy the very necessity for countries to be nations in the first place. And this is the whole idea of making the world a place where territorial boundaries will no longer be necessary.

SECHABA: The leadership of the Black Panther Party has come under very severe attack during the past year. Can you tell us what effects these attacks have had on the Party?

NEWTON: Repression breeds resistance. We feel that by virtue of the fact that we are being attacked, and the attacks are extremely vicious, that we must be hitting a sensitive spot. We have the fascists disturbed and they are running amuck simply because we are threatening them. We are threatening their very foundation, their very existence. Otherwise they would try to pretend to the world that this is democracy and they would support our right to freedom of speech, our right to freedom of the press, and our right to political activity. But all these so-called democratic civil rights are denied the Black Panther Party, which is the vanguard of the people. So the Party must be hitting a sensitive spot; it must be threatening the bureaucratic imperialistic capitalist. We welcome all attacks. We will overcome all obstacles and advance wave upon wave. We will rid the world of the bourgeoisie and destroy all of the monsters, and the whole world will belong to the people.

SECHABA: Do you believe there are revolutionary possibilities in the United States?

NEWTON: I would like to emphasize that without the people of the world struggling against imperialism, we would have a very weak position here in the United States, which I call the urban area of the world. But because we know we have friends, comrades-in-arms who are fighting the same enemy that we are fighting, we feel that what we have done is to open up a new front. We should say we are attempting to open up a new front because we do not claim anything that we haven't done. But we are advancing the fight, we are strengthening our strategy of resistance and attack. We can do this because we realize the American fascist troops are being divided by the people of the world who are struggling against them. We encourage, we admire, we have great admiration for socialist or communist guerrillas all over the world. We feel we will never be free until many colonized people are free. We notice that in most revolutions where a guerrilla-type tactic was used, the urban area or city was the last area to be covered and bases opened up first in the countryside. Now we see many bases opening up in the countryside. We have advanced to the point where in many areas we have gone from a guerrilla to a kind of people's army that can operate with a face to face, head-on collision with the imperialist. This is only because of the great perseverance and great strength that you have shown, and that the people of the world have shown. While we are being attacked from all sides, we are still trying to follow your examples. We realize that you are also being attacked from all sides by the enemy. Because you are driving on you have given us strength to drive on. So onward to victory. We will someday meet and celebrate our victory because I know we will have that. The guerrilla band is our example.

SECHABA: What has been the most important inspiration for the Black Panthers?

NEWTON: I think that not only Fidel and Che, Ho Chi Minh and Mao and Kim II Sung, but also all the guerrilla bands that have been operating in Mozambique and Angola, and the Palestinian guerrillas who are fighting for a socialist world. I think they all have been great inspirations for the Black Panther Party. As I've said before, they're examples of all these guerrilla bands. The guerrillas who are operating in South Africa and numerous other countries all have had great influence on us. We study and follow their example. We are very interested in the strategy that's being used in Brazil, which is an urban area, and we plan to draw on that. And we have certainly been influenced by all of the people who are struggling in the world. As far as control is concerned, our Central Committee controls our Party. But I won't deny the influence. We don't consider that question an accusation because I think we all should learn from each other.

SECHABA: Last year there was a United Front, The National Conference to Combat Fascism, which included a number of groups including SDS, the Dubois Club and the Communist Party of the United States. What is the Black Panther Party policy on this kind of relationship?

NEWTON: Our policy is that we are friends with all Marxists and want coalitions and allies within this country and all over the world. We could never have success without a popular movement, and when I speak of "popular" I mean it in the truest sense of the word, in the internationalist sense. We have to have a popular mass in order to achieve victory because victory is not for us, but the people. Therefore the people must be considered and the people must take a part in the struggle at every level.

We view part of our role as a vanguard is educating the people as we go, orientating them and providing an understanding of the social forces that are in operation and the dialectics at the time. We can only do this through involving the people in practical application, and involving them at every level of the struggle. And we do have relationships and coalitions and just comradely love and work with all these groups, and we hope to even expand this to other groups, some we haven't even heard of yet.

SECHABA: Would the Black Panther Party like to set up or establish more direct contacts with the liberation struggles of Africa, Latin America and Asia?

NEWTON: Yes, we think that we can learn even more from each other if we were to establish better means of communications. One of the chief difficulties is a matter of communications. It is an international struggle. The Black Panther Party even thinks in terms of a new International, an International based upon armed struggle and the socialist ideology. We feel the International that exists now is somewhat deteriorated, as far as the Third World is concerned, especially the Third World countries involved in armed combat. The International has half-stepped and criticized many of the national wars of independence and the armed struggle tactic as being too hasty and without enough orthodox political development. We see the need to overthrow the evil gentry and corrupt officials and we see only one way to do this. We do not believe we can do it through negotiation or electoral politics or any kind of non-violent means. The enemy is a violent man and we must treat him in an appropriate way.

SECHABA: And more specifically, would you be interested in having contact with the liberation movement of Southern Africa and, if so, in what form?

NEWTON: As you know, we have offered troops to the Vietnamese people to show our international solidarity. At the same time we also made it clear that we would send troops or offer troops to any of our friends who would accept them. We think the ultimate gesture of friendship that we could offer is to send our comrades to shed blood on your soil in the name of freedom, in the interest of the people, and against the imperialist enemy. If there is anything else that we can do other than to struggle to break the chains that shackle us, then let us know about that and we will be willing to consider it.

SECHABA: Is there mass interest in the United States about the struggle in Southern Africa? What can *Sechaba* do to publicize the South African revolution among the Black people in the United States?

NEWTON: We, the Black Panther Party, are a vanguard group, so necessarily we are more enlightened than the masses and we are very interested in the international scope of things. The people are as people all over the world, so tied up and so involved in their survival from day to day that much of the time they overlook, or they don't understand, the international nature of the struggle. That is why it is our duty—one of our first duties—to raise the consciousness of the people through education. We would like more information about the struggle in Southern Africa. We are familiar with it right now, but we would like more information on your armed struggle and what the guerrillas are doing so that we can spread this information. We would like film footage. We have trucks that we drive around in the community and show films to people that walk in the streets.

For example, we have films of the revolution that took place in Algeria. The community is very impressed with that kind of thing because they can easily see the relationship between the way the French treated the Algerians and how we are treated in this country. There is an old saying: "A picture is worth a thousand words," and the people perhaps don't read as much as they should, so we found in our political education that it is very helpful to show films. If you have any pictures or film footage you can get to us I will assure you that it will be shown inside of the Black community, the Chinese community, the Indian community, the White community. There are poor White people in this country who are now becoming involved in the common struggle, and we are involved with them. We hope this national kind of involvement of many ethnic groups will aid us in relating to the people and help them make that jump to identify with people in other countries who may be from other ethnic backgrounds, other cultural backgrounds.

Attica Statement:
October 16, 1971

So let it be heard:

A short time ago, the prisoners at Attica requested the Black Panther Party to negotiate with Nixon, Rockefeller and Oswald for their freedom. The Black Panther Party at this time asks Chairman Mao Tse-tung of the People's Republic of China to negotiate with Prison Warden Nixon for the freedom of the oppressed peoples of the world.

We recognize that the criminal activities of trigger-happy Nixon show clearly that he has no respect for peaceful negotiation when the victim is divided and weak. He not only killed the prisoners at Attica but he also murdered his exploited workers, the prison guards. Although most of the prisoners at Attica are Black and all the guards are White, Nixon killed regardless of color, because they were all victims. When the oppressed people of the world ask for negotiation, such as the Vietnamese people, Prison Warden Nixon shows again he has no respect for the people nor his agents, the U.S. Military. HE LEAVES NO ALTERNATIVE BUT VIOLENT, ARMED RESISTANCE. He is responsible for the murder of Vietnamese people and the deaths of the U.S. soldiers. Both the Vietnamese people and the U.S. soldiers are victims of the reactionary Nixon regime. This is why we approached Chairman Mao Tsetung, because we know of his peace-and-freedom-loving nature. There can be no peace without freedom.

We are asking all the agents of Prison Warden Nixon (whom he despises) to join forces with the victims of the world: The U.S. soldiers to join forces with the victimized Vietnamese people; the guards and the families of the deceased guards at Attica and the guards of the state prisons across the U.S. to join forces with the victimized inmates.

It is clear that Mr. Nixon is trigger-happy and could trigger off World War III. And because we knew of his impending visit to the People's Republic of China, we asked the Chinese people to receive us first, so that we might ask the peace-and-freedom-loving Chairman Mao Tse-tung to be the chief negotiator to Mr. Nixon for the peace and freedom of the oppressed peoples of the world. And this is why we ask for unity of all the victims against the common enemy, the Nixon-Rockefeller regime.

So let it be done

Uniting Against the Common Enemy:
October 23, 1971

What does the Black Panther Party mean when we say that we are revolutionary intercommunalists? In a few words, we believe that the world's people form a collection of communities, all dominated or controlled, either directly or indirectly, by the United States, by those few who rule the United States. The most common definition for a nation (as opposed to a community) is a group of human beings who have in common their own land or territory, economic system, culture (or way of day-to-day living), language, etc. At one time men from one nation would go out, and through warfare, conquer other nations. The conquerors would bring under their control the resources, the people, perhaps everything that was sovereign or sacred to the other nation. A variety of things would result: A government of the conquering nation might be established on the territory of the conquered nation; the foreign language may be imposed upon the people; the name of the nation might be changed; or most importantly, the economy of the conquered nation would be fully controlled by the conquerors.

Sometimes a nation is very small; sometimes, very large. But in this way, through these wars, the earth's people have over a very long period of time become divided up according to "national" boundaries, in varying ways at different times in history. These wars of conquest have changed world maps, or what one land mass is called. Sometimes one would look at a certain area and it might have a different name or boundary line, depending upon the date of the map (and sometimes, who printed it). We can remember such terms as the Roman Empire, the Ottoman Empire, the Byzantine Empire. We can remember Columbus "discovering" America (or, as he thought, India); and certainly some changes in national sovereignty have been made since then.

Today, things are different. The entire earth's land mass is known to man. The twentieth century's two World Wars have complicated things even more as to the national question. Technology is so advanced that places about which we had only heard in the past are immediately reachable in person. Today a person can travel completely around the world in less than a day's time. If we bring all these past and present facts together with other information the world begins to look a little different. What else do we need to remember: that in the area of technology, the United States is the most highly advanced country; that a territory as large as China, containing within its boundaries one quarter of the entire earth's population, cannot either lay claim to its own former province, Taiwan, or participate in an organization supposedly representative of all "nations" in the world, the United Nations; that most former empires, such as France, Germany, Italy, Britain, have lost their former holdings (the French have been run out of Vietnam and Algeria; the British, out of India; the Germans, out of Russia and Poland; the Italians, out of Ethiopia, etc.). The point is that only one country stands as the sovereign stronghold, dominating and threatening the sovereignty of all other people and lands—it is the United States Empire. No people, no land, no culture, no national economy is safe from the long arm of the last remaining empire.

The situation is this: A people can look only backwards, to history, to really speak of its nation. We call these former nations communities. All these territories exist under the threat of being brought into or, in fact, being a part of the United States Empire. Some of the territories are liberated, such as China, the northern halves of Korea and Vietnam, or Albania. But the weapons of conquest, the war weapons produced by modern technology, are in the hands of the United States. Not even a liberated territory can lay claim to sovereign control of its land, economy or people with this hanging over its head.

We Black people in the United States have always lived under this threat in our communities inside the United States. United States government control of our communities is not difficult to understand. For most of us it is difficult to imagine our lives without such domination. We have never controlled a land that was ours. We have never controlled our economy. We know of one culture, that as slaves. We know of one language, that of the slavemaster. Our sovereignty was not violated, for we United States Blacks were never a sovereign nation. It is true that we were snatched from African shores. The present fact is that we cannot ask our grandparents to teach us some "native" tongue, or dance or point out our "homeland" on a map. Certainly, we are not citizens of the United States. Our hopes for freedom then lie in the future, a future which may hold a positive elimination of national boundaries and ties; a future of the world, where a human world society may be so structured as to benefit all the earth's people (not peoples).

To achieve this end, we struggle here inside the United States to get rid of our oppression. Others struggle inside their territorial boundaries to get rid of oppression. The more territory we liberate in the world, the closer we will come to an end to all oppression. The common factor that binds us all is not only the fact of oppression but the oppressor: the United States Government and its ruling circle. We, the people of the world, have been brought together under strange circumstances. We are united against a common enemy. Today the philosophy of revolutionary intercommunalism dictates that the survival programs implemented by and with the people here in America and those same basic People's Survival Programs being implemented in Mozambique by the Mozambique Liberation Front are essential to bringing about world unity, from Africa to the Black community inside America, developing and uniting against a common enemy. That enemy has rolled up into one large hand the power of the world. If we get rid of this enemy in a united common struggle it will be easy to transform this unity into a common scheme of things. We are not separate nations of men to continue the pattern of fighting amongst ourselves. We are a large collection of communities who can unite and fight together against our common enemy. The United States' domination over all our territories equals a reactionary (in opposition to the interests of all) set of circumstances among our communities: Reactionary Intercommunalism. We can transform these circumstances to all our benefit: Revolutionary Intercommunalism.

On the continent of Africa there are people who look like us. They are Black. We are brothers because our struggle is common. We have both suffered under White racism and under oppression. This is why we should not let the reactionaries of the world be the only ones communicating across the waters and masses of land. We have a common interest to serve, and therefore, we can learn from each other. What happens here affects our brothers in Africa; what happens in Africa affects us. The United States has seen to this. But this is good. We can learn to fight together, though separated.

There is a place in Africa called Mozambique. It lies on Africa's eastern shore, in the southern portion of the continent. It is a rich land, like most in Africa. In 1498 (six years after Columbus' famous "discovery") the Portuguese invader (if you remember, your elementary school books credit him as an "explorer") Vasco da Gama violated the shores of Mozambique. The rest of the troops landed seven years later, in 1505. From that point on the Portuguese have dominated the economy and lives and the culture of the Mozambican people. Their national language became, and still is, Portuguese. To this day, the Portuguese lay claim to Mozambique, referring to "Portuguese" Mozambique.

This, of course, is not in agreement with our brothers and sisters in Mozambique. Mozambique is their home. They are not the invaders. Of course, the people of Mozambique have made many attempts throughout their long history of Portuguese colonial oppression to rid themselves of their chains. However, the most powerful and successful struggle is presently being waged under the guidance of the revolutionary organization FRELIMO (Front for the Liberation of Mozambique). The people support FRELIMO, for FRELIMO is of the people and is organizing struggle in the true interest of all the people. This great effort really began when FRELIMO was organized in 1962, primarily through the efforts of Dr. Eduardo Mondlane. In 1964 the first attack upon the Portuguese was launched by FRELIMO forces, which were by then organized and trained. Since then, armed struggle has been waged heroically by the Mozambican people under FRELIMO. This has resulted in the liberation of three key areas: Tete Province, Niassa Province and the Mueda Plateau. The ridiculous fact is that the Portuguese deny this. They deny the reality that they will eventually be pushed out of Mozambique (like the United States in Vietnam or in our Black and other oppressed communities). Portuguese Premiere Marcello Caetano (who replaced fascist dictator Salazar) and his "official" Governor General, Eduardo De Oliveira, inside Mozambique, have consistently denied that their troops are being destroyed, their planes shot down.

Caetano denies that FRELIMO membership alone is more than 10,000; that one quarter of Mozambique is liberated territory; that liberated zones have a population of one million people (of a total population of nine million). He wishes to deny the fact that the people are fighting for and winning their freedom. Our brothers in Mozambique know differently. When I was in China earlier this month, I had the opportunity to receive and subsequently report to the people firsthand, accurate information. I met with the President of FRELIMO, Comrade Samora Moises Machel, former Chief of the Army. President Machel gave a clear picture: Not only have three major areas been liberated but FRELIMO has established over 200 primary schools, hospitals and other programs to serve the interest and needs of the people. Recently (in 1968) an entire detachment of women fighters was formed. It was around that time that while denying their losses, the racist, fascist Portuguese government called upon their old friends to help destroy the struggle. In these past two years the United States, Britain, France and Germany have played an openly active role in attempting to destroy the people's struggle for liberation. The United States, of course, "helps" most, providing Boeing-707 planes to bomb the people with napalm and all the other life-destroying material the United States can come up with. President Machel told us that in 1970 alone over 128,000 troops of the combined forces attacked, and 63,000 tons of bombs were viciously rained upon the people. However, President Machel said, "We destroyed the soldiers; we shot down the planes."

These successes have certainly not been easy. From within and from without, the people of Mozambique have suffered. After giving guidance to FRELIMO for nearly seven years, Eduardo Mondlane was assassinated by the enemy. In February of 1969, while in his home (in Tanzania), he opened a box which was part of his morning mail. Upon opening the box a bomb exploded in his face and killed him. Naturally, the Portuguese used even the treachery of this murder to try to deceive the people. Soon after this, Caetano's government issued statements that a "left-wing faction" of FRELIMO had murdered their leader.

As is familiar (or should be to us by now) the Portuguese attempted to install their own "Man" to lead FRELIMO. They tried to push a native Mozambican, Lazaro Kavandame, popular among the people as the leader of the large (200,000 population) Makonde Tribe into leadership of FRELIMO. As a lackey for Portugal, Kavandame began issuing statements like, "Listen to me well. There must not be a single Makonde Chief sending soldiers to war." He was telling the people not to fight for what was theirs. Also, the former Vice-President of FRELIMO, Uriah Simango, was pushing to take over. They were both eventually defeated.

Today, FRELIMO, under the wise leadership of President Machel, is guiding the People of Mozambique toward greater and final victory. But today, naturally, the attacks of the combined forces of the United States, Portugal, Germany, France and Britain are even more fierce: constant bombings and many ground attacks take place. However, there is a more intricate, but ultimately more vicious plan in the making, headed primarily by the United States. They plan to build, for the Portuguese, a large hydroelectric dam. The site for the dam is in the liberated Tete Province in Cabora Bassa, along the Zambesi River, bordering racist Rhodesia. Its purpose is to not only give financial aid to impoverished Portugal but to be used as a key part in a plot with South Africa to lauch a political, diplomatic and military offensive upon all of Africa. A familiar name to us is General Electric. The General Electric Company has spent millions to aid in building the Cabora Bassa Dam. Altogether, the United States and others have agreed to invest 500 million dollars in the dam, which is capable of producing 18.4 billion kilowatts of electricity. Also, in regard to this Cabora Bassa Dam, late FRELIMO President Mondlane once said, "They say it will enable them to settle one million Whites in Mozambique within 10 years . . . to form a great white barrier across Southern Africa."

If we believe that we are brothers with the people of

Mozambique, how can we help? They need arms and other material aid. We have no weapons to give. We have no money for materials. Then how do we help? Or, how can they help our struggle? They cannot fight for us. We cannot fight in their place. We can each narrow the territory that our common oppressor occupies. We can liberate ourselves, learning from and teaching each other along the way. But the struggle is one; the enemy is the same. Eventually, we and our brothers in Mozambique, in all of Africa, throughout the world, can discuss a world without boundaries or national ties. We will have a human culture, a human language, the earth will be all our territory, serving all our interests; serving the interests of all the people.

III

The Bound
and
the Dead

You can kill a revolutionary,
but you can't
kill a revolution—FRED HAMPTON

When a person studies mathematics he learns that there are many mathematical laws which determine the approach he must take to solving the problems presented to him. In the study of geometry one of the first laws a person learns is that "the whole is not greater than the sum of its parts." This means simply that one cannot have a geometrical figure such as a circle or a square which contains more than it does when broken down into smaller parts. Therefore, if all the smaller parts add up to a certain amount the entire figure cannot add up to a larger amount. The prison cannot have a victory over the prisoner because those in charge take the same kind of approach and assume if they have the whole body in a cell that they have contained all that makes up the person. But a prisoner is not a geometrical figure, and an approach which is successful in mathematics is wholly unsuccessful when dealing with human beings.

In the case of the human we are not dealing only with the single individual, we are also dealing with the ideas and beliefs which have motivated him and which sustain him, even when his body is confined. In the case of humanity the whole is much greater than its parts because the whole includes the body which is measurable and confinable and the ideas which cannot be measured nor confined.

The ideas which can and will sustain our movement for total freedom and dignity of the people cannot be imprisoned, for they are to be found in the people, all the people, wherever they are. As long as the people live by the ideas of freedom and dignity, there will be no prison which can hold our movement down. Ideas move from one person to another by the association of brothers and sisters who recognize that a most evil system of capitalism has set us against each other, although our real enemy is the exploiter who profits from our poverty. When we realize such an idea, then we come to love and appreciate our brothers and sisters who we may have seen as enemies, and those exploiters who we may have seen as friends are revealed for what they truly are to all oppressed people. The people are the idea. The respect and dignity of the people, as they move toward their freedom, are the sustaining force which reaches into and out of the prison. The walls, the bars, the guns and the guards can never encircle or hold down the idea of the people. And the people must always carry forward the idea which is their dignity and beauty.

The prison operates with the concept that since it has a person's body it has his entire being, because the whole cannot be greater than the sum of its parts. They put the body in a cell and seem to get some sense of relief and security from that fact. The idea of prison victory, then, is that when the person in jail begins to act, think, and believe the way they want him to, they have won the battle and the person is then "rehabilitated." But this cannot be the case because those who operate the prisons have failed to examine their own beliefs thoroughly, and they fail to understand the types of people they attempt to control. Therefore, even when the prison thinks it has won, there is no victory.

There are two types of prisoners. The largest number are those who accept the legitimacy of the assumptions upon which the society is based. They wish to acquire the same goals as everybody else: money, power, and conspicuous consumption. In order to do so, however, they adopt techniques and methods which the society has defined as illegitimate. When this is discovered such people are put in jail.

They may be called "illegitimate capitalists" since their aim is to acquire everything this capitalistic society defines as legitimate. The second type of prisoner is the one who rejects the legitimacy of the assumptions upon which the society is based. He argues that the people at the bottom of the society are exploited for the profit and advantage of those at the top. Thus, the oppressed exist and will always be used to maintain the privileged status of the exploiters. There is no sacredness, there is no dignity in either exploiting or being exploited. Although this system may make the society function at a high level of technological efficiency, it is an illegitimate system, since it rests upon the suffering of humans who are as worthy and as dignified as those who do not suffer. Thus, the second type of prisoner says that the society is corrupt and illegitimate and must be overthrown. This second type of prisoner is the "political prisoner." They do not accept the legitimacy of the society and cannot participate in its corrupting exploitation, whether they are in the prison or on the block.

The prison cannot gain a victory over either type of prisoner no matter how hard it tries. The "illegitimate capitalist" recognizes that if he plays the game the prison wants him to play he will have his time reduced and be released to continue his activities. Therefore, he is willing to go through the prison programs and say the things the prison authorities want to hear. The prison assumes he is "rehabilitated" and ready for the society. The prisoner has really played the prison's game so that he can be released to resume pursuit of his capitalistic goals. There is no victory, for the prisoner from the "git-go" accepted the idea of the society. He pretends to accept the idea of the prison as a part of the game he has always played.

The prison cannot gain a victory over the political prisoner because he has nothing to be rehabilitated from or to. He refuses to accept the legitimacy of the system and refuses to participate. To participate is to admit that the society is legitimate because of its exploitation of the oppressed. This is the idea which the political prisoner does not accept, this is the idea for which he has been imprisoned, and this is the reason why he cannot cooperate with the system. The political prisoner will, in fact, serve his time just as will the "illegitimate capitalist." Yet the idea which motivated and sustained the political prisoner rests in the people. All the prison has is a body.

The dignity and beauty of man rests in the human spirit which makes him more than simply a physical being. This spirit must never be suppressed for exploitation by others. As long as the people recognize the beauty of their human spirits and move against suppression and exploitation, they will be carrying out one of the most beautiful ideas of all time. Because the human whole is much greater than the sum of its parts. The ideas will always be among the people. The prison cannot be victorious because walls, bars and guards cannot conquer or hold down an idea.

Eulogy for Jonathan Jackson and William Christmas: August 15, 1970*

While it is viewed as a tragedy and many would weep for Jonathan Jackson and William A. Christmas, the Black Panther Party serves notice that it is not brothers Jonathan Jackson and William A. Christmas for whom we should weep. They have achieved freedom and we remain slaves. If we must weep let it be for those of us who remain in bondage.

The Black Panther Party will follow the example that was set by these courageous revolutionaries. The people refuse to submit to the slavery and bondage that is required in order to live a few more years on the planet earth. IF THE PENALTY FOR THE QUEST FOR FREEDOM IS DEATH, THEN BY DEATH WE ESCAPE TO FREEDOM.

Without freedom life means nothing. We have nothing to lose but our shackles and freedom to gain. We have gathered today not only to give respect to Comrades Jonathan Jackson and William Christmas, but also to pledge our lives to the accomplishment of the goals exemplified in their actions.

THERE ARE NO LAWS THAT THE OPPRESSOR MAKES THAT THE OPPRESSED ARE BOUND TO RESPECT.

Laws should be made to serve people. People should not be made to serve laws. When laws no longer serve the

---

* At St. Augustine's Church, Twenty-Seventh and West Streets, Oakland, California.

people, it is the people's right and the people's duty to free themselves from the yoke of such laws.

Oppressed people in general, and Black people in particular, have suffered too long and we must draw the line somewhere. There is a big difference between thirty million unarmed Black people and thirty million Black people armed to the teeth.

We are not alone. We have allies everywhere. We find our comrades wherever in the world we hear the oppressor's whip. People all over the world are rising up. The high tide of revolution is about to sweep the shores of America, sweeping away the evil gentry and corrupt officials.

Our comrades Jonathan Jackson and William A. Christmas have taught us a revolutionary lesson. They have intensified the struggle and placed it on a higher level.

A picture is worth a thousand words, but action is supreme, Comrades Jonathan Jackson and William A. Christmas have made the ultimate sacrifice. They have given the revolution their lives.

Lonnie McLucas and the New Haven 9: August 29, 1970

HOWARD*: This press conference is to announce a mass demonstration rally that we are going to hold on the New Haven Green starting Tuesday, August 25. This is in relationship to the ending of the trial of Lonnie McLucas. The trial will end Tuesday, August 25, and we will hold a mass rally, demonstration and a vigil until the jury comes to a verdict. You can ask your questions then. We have the Minister of Defense, Supreme Commander, and the leader of our Party here. He'll respond to your questions.

NEWTON: First, I'd like to say it is very important that the community come out to support the rally because only with the power of the people are we able to achieve justice or to receive justice. The only reasons that the courts made a concession on my case and let me out on bail is because of the power of the people. It is not because of the justice of the court. So we are calling for the community to support all political prisoners and prisoners of war. At this time, the racist reactionary government is about to commit a legal lynching on Lonnie McLucas and the New Haven 9, and we are asking the community to come and issue a mandate against this. We were informed by McLucas that he was offered a deal by the district attorney. Whenever there is a serious case against a person and there is really substantial evidence, no deal is offered. McLucas was offered a sentence of fifteen to twenty years with a guarantee he would

* Captain of New Haven Headquarters of the Black Panther Party, New Haven, Conn.

be out in eight. They offered him this only if he would testify against everyone else, including our Chairman Bobby Seale, Landon Williams and Ericka Huggins because these are the people they really want. So, they are willing to make any sort of deal because they know that they don't have any evidence on anyone because everyone is innocent. But if they could use that old tactic of divide and conquer then they would simply try to divide our Party members against each other, pay them off, and have a legal lynching based upon some testimony coming from one of our comrades. But, of course, none of the Party members will go for this. Only the ones who are agents will go for it, such as Sams who is the only murderer and who's already accepted the deal. But we think that what has happened is that the F.B.I. used Sams as an agent and then dumped him. They have a history of doing this and they will do it again, it seems.

The rally will be at 10:00 A.M. on Tuesday, August 25, and we are asking everyone to stay until the verdict comes in. The jury goes out Tuesday evening or Wednesday morning. We're asking everyone to stay until the end and to mobilize the community against this legal lynching.

We're very concerned about what's happening now in America as far as the persecution of prisoners of war. The revolutionary movement is reaching a very decisive level. We're demanding that the powers that be in this country follow the Geneva Agreement relating to prisoners of war. They have no right to inflict any punishment on a prisoner of war. They are required to keep him until we negotiate for his release, and they have no right to brutalize him and they surely have no right to murder him. If they try to do this the people can only take appropriate actions, and we are convinced that we will only get justice when the people start acting in a revolutionary manner. I think it's unnecessary to go into exactly what the tactics should be. I think our actions should speak for themselves. If we are really going to take some genuine revolutionary actions we don't have to talk about them. The Panthers have a maxim that says: "To say what I want to say, I can't do what I want to do, and to do what I want to do, I can't say what I want to say." So, just observe my actions and you'll know what I want to say. We will observe this maxim and in the very near future you'll see some very revolutionary action. But this will happen only if we can mobilize the community behind us. So I emphasize this not to be redundant but just to impress upon you the absolute necessity to educate the community. In spite of the revolutionary action we, the vanguard group, take, it is still necessary to educate the community by any means necessary. This includes using tactics which may appear reformist but which in fact are not. I say they're not reformist because any action taken in the community that won't impede the future revolutionary goal is appropriate action, whether it is a medical program or a child care center, or whatever. Whatever the community needs, we should be there to serve them. Serve the people!

PRESS: What's going to happen if McLucas is found guilty? Do you have any plans?

NEWTON: First thing, we want the people who are there to issue the mandate against this conviction. We don't think he is going to be convicted because there is no evidence against him. If injustice is done we will take measures to correct this and institute justice, revolutionary justice. As I said before, I don't think that it's necessary to discuss tactics, especially if these tactics might be military tactics. If we have to engage in military tactics it won't be for political reasons because we're not playing any games. We want our comrades free and we want all political prisoners set free as well as prisoners of war.

PRESS: Would you answer a question I think a lot of White people have had? They say that Alex Rackley has been shot and they feel that there should have been an arrest of at least someone in connection with the killing and a trial. How do you feel about that?

NEWTON: In the first place I don't endorse the reactionary racist courts. I don't think they should deal with any of the people because they haven't earned that right. I think that the community should make rules to revolutionize its judicial system and handle its own problem. The community's problem is the judicial system. It is the judicial system that is the problem, not the people, just as the prison problem is not the prisoner. The real problem is the prison authorities. The prison administration needs to be separated and isolated for their racism and their reactionary attitudes. We contend that the prisons are not rehabilitation centers; they are concentration camps where racism is practiced and encouraged by the prison administration. They use the lack of social consciousness of the prisoners to institute this racism, therefore you have the race wars inside the prisons. I think this kind of thing is ending now because prisoners are more and more taking action against the real enemy. As far as this particular case, where Rackley was killed, he certainly should not have been killed. He was a member of the Black Panther Party in good standing. George Sams should be dealt with; he should have to stand before a revolutionary court. I don't even wish the reactionary racist courts upon George Sams. It hasn't improved him. He's been in and out of penitentiaries all his life. He has spent most of his life between going to mental institutions and prisons. As far as I'm concerned, George Sams is a madman and true revolutionary justice in his case would be putting him in a therapeutic environment. The only problem is that we don't have a therapeutic environment in the world today because of United States imperialism—bureaucratic capitalism at home and imperialism abroad. So what we have to do is move in such a fashion that we'll transform this society and therefore transform the world, and then we'll have a society where we can help madmen and where we could really develop all human beings to their highest level.

PRESS: Do you have a revolutionary court system now, other than the Central Committee, that would handle this sort of situation?

NEWTON: At this point we can't really talk about any revolutionary institutions. We can talk about a process that is in the making. We have a provisional revolutionary judicial system which we realize can't function to its greatest capacity. Because you can't have isolated pockets of human treatment when reaction is pressing in all around you. So we don't claim to have developed any utopia in our commune system in which we live or in the Party itself. We have problems because we exist in a backward society. So we know our chief task at this point is to transform the society. It's not simply to erect just institutions because it's impossible to do that either in this country or in the world as a whole, today, until reaction, and that consists of the seventy-six companies that control the world, is killed once and for all.

On the Capture of Angela Davis: October 17, 1970

The Black Panther Party accuses the reactionary authorities of California and the United States of using Angela Davis as a scapegoat. The traditional judiciary are responsible for the event that took place in the Marin Courtroom, and the police are responsible for the murder of the judge, Jonathan Jackson, William Christmas and James McClain, as well as the wounding of the hostages. In order to draw attention from the responsible persons Angela Davis was hunted, captured, and accused of crimes of which the American reactionary system is in fact guilty of.

The event would have not taken place if there were justice in the courts for Black people. The court has been generally nonresponsive to the cries for redress of Black people's grievances and have continued to act in the interest of the racist, capitalist ruling circle. This is clear when we note that the prosecuting attorney in the Marin case is married to the niece of the judge who presided over the case. On the other hand, Jonathan Jackson and the prisoners of war, William Christmas, James McClain and Ruchell Magee, were motivated by their desire for justice and freedom. We feel that when all peaceful means are exhausted, it is the people's right, it is the people's duty, to take other steps that will guarantee justice and freedom.

The San Quentin guards and the Marin County police must be charged with the murders of Comrades Jackson, McClain and Christmas and the murder of the judge. We note that absolutely no one in the establishment has made issue of the fact that all of the shots fired in the Marin incident came from the vicious weapons of the police and the district attorney. It is clear that the gestapo police were not interested in the preservation of human life. Their first concern was apprehension and murder, and if anyone happened to survive, this would be an accident and not their chief concern. It shows that the gestapo are not even concerned about the lives of their class brothers, the judge and the district attorney.

So it seems that absolute madness has swept the shores of America. Reason is not to be found among the ranks of the oppressor. The very fact that the reactionary authority has the audacity to accuse Angela Davis of a crime is indicative of the lack of justice and the lack of simple reasoning. Those who are clearly guilty are exonerated. Those who are victims and innocent stand accused.

The Black Panther Party calls upon Black people in particular and all oppressed people in general to rise up and do whatever is necessary to free Angela Davis. Angela Davis has exemplified the highest expression of concern for the people. We the people should show our appreciation of this by coming to her aid in this hour of need. Angela has given her energy and devotion to the people's cause without reference to her personal safety, without reference to her personal gain. She has given in a free and a very pure way, in a way that sets an example for people everywhere. We must not fail Angela Davis.

Eulogy for Samuel Napier:
May 1, 1971

There is very much in my heart today. And I have very few words to express it. Samuel L. Napier was one of the first brothers to join the Black Panther Party, and therefore he is a veteran of the struggle. He had always been attached to distribution of our paper, the Black Panther paper, which is the life of the Party. The voice of the people. Those who would cut off Samuel Napier would cut off the voice of the people. But because the voice is manifested in all of us, collectively, the voice will go on.

Death comes to all of us, but it varies in its significance. To die for the reactionaries, the racists, the capitalists is lighter than a feather. But to die in the service to the people is heavier than any mountain and deeper than any sea. Samuel's death is very significant. He will live on in spirit because we will make sure that we will advance the struggle. And we will cry for those who are living because we are in very bad shape. Samuel has now put down his burden; and it will be very heavy for us because he carried the burden for thousands. He was an extremely hard worker. We won't be able to replace him. No. We can only fill in the ranks with a hundred, with a thousand men.

Samuel Napier was a servant of the people; he gave the supreme gift to the people. So therefore Samuel Napier was the Supreme Servant of the people.

The dismissal of the case by the State of Connecticut against our Chairman Bobby Seale and our Comrade Ericka Huggins is a clear indication that the might and power of the people is beginning to show. That the judge in New Haven was forced to say, "It is humanly impossible to find a jury," means several things: the State was not willing to spend another several million dollars, a retrial would be so obscene as to cause an even greater and louder demand from the people for Bobby and Ericka's freedom than ever before, and that nowhere could a jury of twelve people be found that would bring back a conviction.

We certainly will be glad to welcome Bobby and Ericka back among us, but we are not so foolish as to allow this compromise to cloud our vision. Bobby and Ericka will be back among the people, but they are not free, the people are not free, and there are hundreds more political prisoners: George Jackson and the Soledad Brothers, Ruchell Magee, Angela Davis, and all the unknowns, all the Black and poor people viciously incarcerated right now in this country's maximum security camps. Also there are the masses of oppressed people throughout the world that are still suffering under the direct or indirect boot of oppression from the U.S. ruling circle.

It is the power of the people and the people only to whom we will be thankful, and in whom our faith rests for the future. Bobby and Ericka have spent two long years in isolated and barbarous prisons. Nothing will justify those years except the victory of the people, Black people, poor people and all the oppressed people of the world over the fascist, imperialist U.S. empire.

REVOLUTIONARY SUICIDE

HUEY P. NEWTON

- INITIALLY PUBLISHED IN 1973 BY HARCOURT BRACE, THIS AUTOBIOGRAPHY SERVED AS THE PRIMARY SOURCE FOR THE MANY BOOKS WRITTEN ABOUT HUEY P. NEWTON.

- PROFILES BLACK PANTHER LEADERS, INCLUDING BOBBY SEALE, ELDRIDGE CLEAVER, KATHLEEN CLEAVER, ELAINE BROWN, AND DAVID HILLIARD.

In October 1967, one year after the founding of the Black Panther Party, Huey Newton was involved in a shooting during which an Oakland police officer was killed. Newton spent three years in prison before being released and having his charges dismissed., and is jailing brought cries of "Free Huey" from supporters around the world.

This engrossing and well-written autobiography recounts the forming of a revolutionary and shows how the degrading and psychologically destructive penal system forged Newton's already growing spirit.

Huey Newton is as intelligent and charismatic on paper as he was in person, and his autobiography serves as bold testimony tot he ideas that formed the Black Panther movement in the 1960s and '70s and that are being aired and reconsidered today.

HUEY P. NEWTON, founder of the Black Panther Party and its chief theoretician, has long been a hero to radicals and is currently being rediscovered by young people interested in the history of black power in the United States.

$14.95 ($20.95 Canada), Trade paper. ISBN 0-86316-326-2, 250 pp, 6 x 9. 24 B&W photos

Writers and Readers

WRITERS AND READERS PUBLISHING, INC.